SCREENWRITING FUNDAMENTALS

Screenwriting Fundamentals: The Art and Craft of Visual Writing is a workshop in a book that takes a step-by-step approach to screenwriting, starting from a blank page and working through the book to a first draft. Written in a style that's direct and easy to understand, it is full of humor and valuable insights. Building incrementally through the basic elements of the craft, Bauer gives strong emphasis to the ever-present camera and the subsequent importance of Visual Writing. The second half of the book focuses on the narrative and dramatic aspect of screenwriting and the emotional and visual logic required in developing the script from an original idea into a writer's Treatment and on to the full finished First Draft. Irv Bauer puts the pieces together and takes the process out of the cerebral and into the immediate do-as-you-go practical approach. He focuses the writer's skills and encourages the use of the writer's imagination throughout the book. In addition, the many examples, both his own and his students', provide ample stimulus and guidance at every stage of the process.

This book features

- A unique emphasis on the visual elements of storytelling because the camera is always present—the screenplay must act as a guide for the director and the editor.
- A "workshop in a book" approach that walks the reader step-by-step through a screenplay—focusing on character, location, time frame, visual components, and transitions—with plenty of exercises that generate material for the narrative writing process.
- A process-oriented approach, combined with a lighthearted tone and approachable style, that allows the reader to ease into the daunting task of writing a First Draft and takes them all the way through to the end—First Draft in hand.

Irv Bauer's vast experience in teaching screenwriting includes undergraduate programs at New York University and Sarah Lawrence College, playwriting at many universities and venues, and non-performance workshops for writers at the New Dramatists. Irv is the author of several produced and optioned plays and screenplays as well as many commissioned rewrites for film and television and for the stage. Bauer wrote Season 1 of the animated series *Courage The Cowardly Dog* and was Senior Story Consultant on all four seasons. Bauer has mentored countless up-and-coming industry writers and directors and conducted his own very successful classes and tutorials that have drawn students from all over the world.

Irv Bauer is a force. An inspiration in teaching, he challenges the story at its deepest emotional level.

Brad Furman, Director/Screenwriter,
The Lincoln Lawyer, Los Angeles

Irv inspired me and opened a whole new world to me. His clear structure and sharp understanding of the craft is peerless.

Grit Fischer, Graduate, Hochschule Film School, Berlin

Irv Bauer's screenwriting course was a huge benefit to me at the start of my career as an independent film producer. I was able to gain a fresh perspective on how to look at a script and understand what makes it good or bad. Irv has a simple and effective method of developing characters and story, and translating ideas into properly written, comprehensive screenplays. Once you learn and understand his process, you can easily see in a script where some of those fundamentals are solid or lacking.

Steve Shapiro, Producer, *November Man,*
Into The Forest, Winter's Bone, New York/Los Angeles

When I was a student at NYU, and later as well, Irv Bauer not only taught me about the craft of screenwriting he also helped me find and shape my own voice. He taught me the importance of creativity and originality, and turning out material that resonates with the heart. Irv is truly my mentor and I'll always value him as my teacher.

Meng Ong, Director/Screenwriter, *A Fantastic*
Ghost Wedding, Miss Wonton, Singapore

I think of Irv often especially when I read scripts. "What would Irv think and suggest here?" He helps me a lot. I owe him a lot.

Luigi Ferrara-Santamaria, Producer, Rome

We must undo what we think we know in order to be in the embrace of Irv's wisdom, a real privilege and a great surprise! He walked me through the dark tunnel of writer's block. Irv Bauer's process and intimate hands on experience of screen writing, comes from a lifetime. "I am the lucky one!"

Joanne Cheng, Director/Screenwriter, *Bound Feet,*
C/O Butterfly, Beijing/New York

Irv was my screenwriting teacher at NYU in the 90s. Later, I studied with him privately. His deeply rooted passion to character development and storytelling was and will always be an inspiration to me. They don't make them like Irv anymore.

Evan Footman Kreeger

Irv Bauer is a powerful antidote to the Hollywood meat grinder school of screenwriting. You won't find pat templates, or tired plot-by-numbers schematics, but a unique method combining the tools working writers have been utilizing for centuries, all presented in concise, easy steps. Irv helped me reclaim that sine qua non of all successful writers—passion.

Stephen Beckner, Writer/Director, Paris

A master teacher, Irv Bauer has the rare ability to break down the craft of screenwriting into an understandable step by step process. Extremely knowledgeable, Bauer synthesizes his many years of experience, giving students the tools they need to develop their work from character sketch to finished screenplay. A dynamic and inspiring approach that yields extremely gratifying results.

Eileen Kurtis-Kleinman, Student,
Sarah Lawrence College, New York

Kudos for Irv Bauer's screenwriting course. It definitely ain't a bombastic, boring lecture. It's a hands-on, minds-on, writing process. It is said that if you want to learn to write you have to write. They coined this expression for Irv's course and he makes it fun.

Robert E. Lee, Screenwriter, Editor/Writer,
Long Beach Style Magazine, New York

I completed a BFA at New York University Film School and I hold Irv largely responsible for my success in my career, without him I would be in a totally different place. I cannot complement Irv Bauer enough on his help, humor and style of teaching. He made script writing fun.

Martin Kovel, Producer/Director, Sydney, Australia

Irv Bauer is the best hands-on screenwriting teacher in the business. He doesn't dictate. He knows that every work is different. His experience and guidance elevated my work.

Robert K. Wilcox, Author, Journalist, Screenwriter, Editor

Irv Bauer takes screenwriting out of the cerebral and puts it into the practical. I hear from people about all of these "famous" screenwriting gurus. I've also read some of their books. While well written they're mostly academic and theoretical in concept but not much help when figuring out how to apply on to the page. That's where Irv's process outshines them all.

Carlotta Schoch, Actress, Screenwriter, Producer,
Los Angeles/New York

SCREENWRITING FUNDAMENTALS

The Art and Craft of Visual Writing

Irv Bauer

Compiled and Edited by Vimi Bauer

Routledge
Taylor & Francis Group

NEW YORK AND LONDON

First published 2017
by Routledge
711 Third Avenue, New York, NY 10017

and by Routledge
2 Park Square, Milton Park, Abingdon, Oxon OX14 4RN

Routledge is an imprint of the Taylor & Francis Group, an informa business

Part Divider Graphic: Student sketch of Irv Bauer mid-session: Greg Polk

Library of Congress Cataloging in Publication Data
Names: Bauer, Irv, –2015 author. | Bauer, Vimi compiler editor.
Title: Screenwriting fundamentals : the art and craft of visual writing / Irv Bauer ; compiled and edited by Vimi Bauer.
Description: New York : Routledge, 2016. | Includes bibliographical references and index.
Identifiers: LCCN 2016027256 | ISBN 9781138666214 (hardback : alk. paper) | ISBN 9781138666221 (pbk. : alk. paper) | ISBN 9781315619507 (e-book)
Subjects: LCSH: Motion picture authorship. | Motion picture plays—Technique.
Classification: LCC PN1996 .B385 2016 | DDC 808.2/3—dc23
LC record available at https://lccn.loc.gov/2016027256

ISBN: 978-1-138-66621-4 (hbk)
ISBN: 978-1-138-66622-1 (pbk)
ISBN: 978-1-315-61950-7 (ebk)

Typeset in Sabon
by Apex CoVantage, LLC

Contents

Editor's Note

There is something I want to share with you. My husband of 35 years, Irv Bauer, died suddenly last year, just prior to the period he had set aside to write this book. Heartbroken, I reached out to the publishers, who, in an extraordinary leap of faith, contracted me, Irv's wife—and also collaborator, co-producer, and teaching assistant—to write the book and extended the deadline by three months. I have followed Irv's detailed book proposal, which was to impart the material as he taught it in his classes and seminars in a framework of ten sessions. The task of finding, gathering, selecting, and compiling and editing the material, though enormous, has been a labor of love. A gift for which I will be ever grateful.

My deepest gratitude goes to the editor Emily McCloskey for believing in the project from the start with Irv and then supporting me all the way through. I also want to thank Julie Strong, a former student who later became a devoted friend, as many did, for encouraging and supporting me in the decision to take on writing the book; and Sam, for his contribution. Then there's Erin Koster! Amazing Erin's tireless efforts helped keep the material organized through two rewrites and multiple shifts in ideas. With all my best intentions, without these four people there would be no book.

Lastly, to the students! Irv's unbounded gratitude and appreciation for their allowing him to use a few of their exercises is shared by me tenfold. Without their contribution, the book would not be as rich. Thank you Luiz Antonio, Dovid, Johanne, Mark, Sue, Jessica, Nur, Anja, Juha, Sabina, Donata, Suzi, Andre, Carmen, and Sophia. I am in your debt for life, and please know, as you do, that all your work is protected by copyright. There are many other students, too, who brought Irv satisfaction over the years, in showing their respect and appreciation for him and for what he taught them. The comment most frequently expressed by the students and professionals Irv guided and taught over the years was that he helped them think. He had extraordinary clarity and logic, and he helped them focus on the essentials. "Take the water out," he would say. What identified his teaching, too, was the emphasis on the visual. People remarked that working with him was the catalyst in their transformation from being a writer to being a screenwriter.

Irv Bauer believed strongly that having a process to rely on is invaluable and essential to becoming a professional writer. He cautioned writers: "The common practice of 'writing what comes next' is like driving in the dark. You may get there, you may not . . . and you most certainly will waste a lot of time." This book is a compilation of notes Irv made specifically for it, along with comments, notes, and other material from his lectures and classroom instruction at universities, his presentations to media people all over the world, and his private group classes and tutorials. The book, in its truest sense, is a writer speaking to other writers.

The key elements of the craft of screenwriting are introduced in the first part of the book with an exercise at the end of each chapter. Starting with an arbitrary character and situations, nothing previously considered, no preconceived notions or ideas, writers understand each element as a stand-alone component of the overall craft. At the early stage of learning a new process, the freshness of the endeavor is all important and writers are advised to suspend judgment and analysis and enjoy the freedom to play. The imagination is a powerful tool. Some access it easier than others; but as a screenwriter, it is indispensable.

The second part of this book emerges from the subjects of a second semester at universities. This is where the writer proves out the nuts and bolts learned and practiced in the first part or semester. When divided like that, the second semester requires the writer, having on their own completed the prewriting phase, use this stage as a starting point where they then can prove out the craft—and the art—of the entire process of screenwriting. The combined sections provide a foundation, a blueprint that can be relied on for writing short narrative films or full-length feature films. The close to forty examples taken from the author's own scripts as well as examples of students' work are there to illustrate and amplify the process and to support the writer through their progress.

Between the covers of this book you have the fundamentals, the toolbox, the skill-set that Irv Bauer used all the years of his professional writing life and that will serve and hopefully guide and stimulate the writer. My hope, as was Irv's, is that you will continue to refer to the book even after you have completed the course and avail of Irv's guidance to stimulate you and push you past the inevitable stale moments.

Being a born dramatist, Irv Bauer wrote as he spoke, whether in his screenplays, his stage plays, his articles, or as a film and theater critic. The book is therefore written in the first person, in his voice and compiled from the years of material I had access to—not the least of which is Irv's voice, alive in my head forever.

Vimi Bauer
New York, 2016

**It is important to be aware that the examples in the book are not the final versions, but works in process in draft form, and they have been retained as such for authenticity.

Foreword

Irv Bauer was a very special man, both creative and generous in all he did. Always at hand to talk, discuss, his font of knowledge on his craft was endless and fascinating. I would sit and listen to him for hours. This book is testament to his achievements and his influence on others' lives.

Michael Radford
London, May 2016

INTRODUCTION
On Being a Writer

There is a barrage of information on film available. Up-to-date technology has put an affordable camera into the hands of every dreamer. The computer rules. Software gives you formatting, jazzy editing, and now even mix-and-match characters. You crowdfund the project and—bingo—a digital world is at your fingertips. Creativity has been democratized. We are all budding geniuses. And why not? However, I can't tell you how many times I've had people call me saying they have just completed this or that course or seminar, or received a degree in film, but they have a hole in their knowledge when it comes to screenwriting. They have been given the information and a general understanding but nothing hands-on, so they don't really even know where to begin.

Many budding writers say, "I'm serious about my writing. I work every morning from six to eight. I set that time aside and I write!" Or, "Seven to nine in the evening, I have a quick bite and I sit down at my computer and I write!" Putting words on the page alone does not make you a writer. Granted, it is way ahead of the many beginning writers whom I hear say, "Oh, it's in my head." The act of writing is of utmost importance, but before you get to that point, before the physical act of putting it on the page, there is the matter of Time.

The rush of an idea is exciting, almost intoxicating, but it is only the beginning. So the first thing I'd like to talk about is Time. Time in the context of what it means to a writer and to writing. Our world has sped up to the point of no return. "I've got the idea, I've got the story. Bang! It's finished. Here it is." We live in a very hectic world. . . . We're very busy. We are also very sophisticated now. The promise of instant gratification is tucked into our subconscious at every turn. But I'm saying that as writers we are challenged to ignore that track and instead find our own counter rhythm and flow. It takes time to write like your unique self.

Prewriting

So, Time. Time in the context of what it means to a writer and to writing. What I'm talking about more specifically is the prewriting time. What does that mean? It means making the time . . . for the prewriting time. It means time to let our subconscious help us. That may sound pretentious; it's not. Time for contemplation. Time for gestation. We have to allow time for the dreaming that we do. The walking-around dreaming, the dreaming at night . . . either before we go to sleep, or while asleep, when our subconscious helps us . . . throws up some stuff for us to think about before we get out of bed in the morning. Time. Time in and around everything else you do. On your way to work. Washing the dishes. Fixing the car. Time to think about the character you may write about or whatever idea is germinating in your head. Nothing may come to you, or you may connect with something.

Time spent outside the results-oriented norm. Time to contemplate, time to consider, time to dream . . . because the dreaming really, in a funny way, is what it is all about. Time to generate material to create the whole cloth, out of which you will eventually cut the pattern and write your story.

When you've seen a film that has engaged you, that you've enjoyed, have you stopped to think about all the things the writer needed to find out about in order to fill those two hours that held your interest? A feature film is about two hours; a short film can be ten to twenty minutes, on average. Either way, proportionately, that is the amount of material you will need. A lot of material. A lot of time. If you say you haven't got the time, it is likely you will never reach the full potential of your intention. So Time is something to consider seriously.

What Does Being a Writer Mean?

Earlier I mentioned that putting it on the page is of utmost importance, and it is. Yes—even before we get to writing the first draft of the script—in the prewriting stage, we have to cultivate the habit of writing down all the fragments of ideas and dialogue and suggestions that come to us in and around everything we do each day. Some will be short notes, a word, a line or two; some will be long, a paragraph or more. Write it down. Do not rely on your memory to be your ally. Joan Didion, the acclaimed American novelist and essayist, quoted her husband John Gregory Dunne, also a novelist, as saying, "Making a note as and when it comes to you is the difference between writing and not writing."

In the early stages of my life as a writer, I used to write on anything. Yet I always found there was an overflow. I would go outside, or go to dinner, or do something else, and the ideas would keep coming. So I'd write on napkins, I'd write on pieces of paper, I'd write on an actor's book, I would write on the back of a bill. I would write on anything that was in my pocket. One day, walking down the street, all of a sudden I got two lines of dialogue, terrific dialogue, for this piece I was working on. Reached into my pocket. Not only didn't I have a piece of paper—I must have changed my pants—no paper, no pen, no pencil, nothing. I panicked!

I realized, then, that there's got to be a better way to capture this material that spills out. I have these little 3 × 5 spiral-bound notebooks. I buy them in bulk. I carry them around with me in my back pocket or my shirt pocket. I give them to all my students; I hand them out. A small detail: I number them on the covers, as 1, 2, 3, and so on.

You must have immediate access to a notebook at all times. Collect material, write it down, and fill the books up because your memory—you can't trust it, so writing it down as soon as you get it is critical. Especially with dialogue. As you'll find out later, dialogue is all about rhythms. You've got to write the words down in the way that you hear them in your head, or heard them in conversation, or on the street in passing. Not the idea of what the words mean, but the specific words in the specific order because you won't remember it that way later, unless you write it down. Write it in your notebook so you've captured it.

So you see, the prewriting phase is as important as the writing phase because when you start writing your script you are writing out of a collection of material you've already gathered; you're not making it up as you go. I call it the Gathering Phase, the collection bag phase . . . whatever. You write down everything connected with some aspect of the material because you don't know what's going to be important later and what's not going to be important later, so you take everything. You can't have too much information to get started.

I am convinced that preparation is the key to writing a successful screenplay. The connections to the material that you forge deep inside yourself *before* you are ready to write. All that fluff and stuff you find during the Gathering Phase. You need to prime the pump and let it all gush out in its own way and in its own time in the service of preparing you to write the screenplay.

In order to fully understand the process, in this book we are going to work with a certain limited amount of information: material that will be generated in the exercises that you do after reading each chapter. You'll have a character to work with. You'll have locations to work with. You'll have situations that begin to develop. Anything and everything goes into the notebook to help you when you get to the writing part. You have to commune with the material that is inside of yourself and all the fleeting observations you make of things you see and hear. All the fragments that come out of your imagination. You have to make those very deep inner connections with the material, so that afterwards you won't be writing off the surface, off the top of your head, "what comes next." You will write your script out of an abundance of material that will propel you into a richness from which to tell your story in a unique way.

When I first started writing, I thought, like everybody else, that the division between the research (whatever that meant) and the writing was 10 percent research and 90 percent writing. Now, after all these years, the balance has shifted from 10/90 to 70/30. Seventy percent of the time is for the research—for this contemplative work, the discovery phase, this prewriting phase, the gathering of material of all sorts, in every direction, in every shading. Once I know what I am writing, once I know what the material is, once I know what that cloth is, what the pattern is that I will cut out of that cloth, the writing part is easy. The writing part is easy because it has been practiced and practiced in this initial phase, and I'm comfortable. The material and I are on intimate terms. I'm confident with it now. I know right from the start of a project that I've got to generate the material and connect with the material in order for the material to then come back to me when I'm writing and flow and be something that's rich and interesting with its own individuality. Not derivative, not formulaic, but original.

This is as good a place as any to emphasize a much-misunderstood part of being a writer. A lot of writers are, at heart, researchers. The digging up of background material, information, is what many enjoy. By research, I mean, yes, necessary facts, accuracy, but the prewriting time is as much and more about the discovery process. The two are not to be confused. Facts matter little in fiction except for the sake of accuracy. Discover all the shades and colors that the compost heap of your imagination generates in and around the facts and the information that you uncover. It is the amalgam that feeds your story.

We often cheat ourselves; we don't allow ourselves time, and we end up chasing the story. Being a writer does not make you a better person. But if you are going to spend that time of your life writing, if that's something that you are going to do seriously, then know what you are doing and how to do it.

Craft, my friends, craft. Craft and practice. Yes, like the man who stops to ask, "How do you get to Carnegie Hall?" The stranger replies, "Practice, practice, practice." And, I'd add, "individuality." The only thing we've got going for us is our own individuality. But we have to trust ourselves. We have to give ourselves permission to get to that place where our own unique voice is heard. We have to access that self. Not easy. You've got to go into yourself; you've got to make the inner connections, and that takes Time. It is from the wellspring of that inner self that you write.

When negotiating contracts with my lawyers, yes, I am concerned with how much money I am going to get, but it's not the primary factor. For me, it's "How much time will I have?" I want my lawyer, my agents, my representatives to get me as much time as they can. That's a big factor for me in the negotiations: How much time can I get? Because I know I will need it all and I will use it all. Time. Time is required. Time is necessary. Time is intrinsic to the value of the work you do. Time. As writers, we spend a lot of time alone, and you must be prepared to do that. But we are never actually alone because we have all these characters running around in our heads. Some may say we're a little crazy. Maybe. But good crazy.

So we'll begin our work together with the prewriting phase. All the basic elements that go into the Gathering Phase. It's where we collect the material, find the choice bits, the little gems or big moments that, worked in later, will eventuate in the screen story. The phase that generates the material that propels us into story.

Historically—and I mean in all the workshops and teaching I've done—the stories work. Some work less well than others, but they all work. Doing good work involves a process. The prime concern here is not to write a masterpiece; it is to understand the process, the logic of why and how you do what you do in approaching story. Note—very important—that I say "approaching" story. Bear with me, we'll get to story, I promise you. How do you make the choices that you make? Take my word for it that it's not a matter of common sense. It's not a matter of I'll write it until I get it right. You may never get it right. It involves making copious notes; it involves gathering more material than you will actually use. It involves dreaming. And (I can't stress this enough) it involves your imagination. It requires an investment of yourself. Allow for your emotions to help you in the writing. We are not journalists, we are not reporters, we are not making documentaries—although this approach will help you in those pursuits as well.

Let's begin.

PART I

THE GATHERING PHASE

ONE

Character, Location, Time Frame

When you are working in the real world, you may start with a rough idea. You may start with a situation that seems worthy. You may start with a commission for a story and be given the premise. If you're lucky, you'll start with a character that has tickled your interest. Whatever the case, when you find your character, you will find your story—not the other way round. Character is of prime importance because it is the characters of our imagination that we evolve, that we create, that carry OUR ideas . . . our ideas, alive, to the audience.

These characters deliver our message, make our arguments, present our puzzles, and give voice to the humor, drama, perplexity, and mystery of what it means to be human. Our characters allow us to make our, the writer's, concerns and insights theirs, the audience's. Creatures of our imagination and human research, they are our representatives, our conduits. As such, they must be believable, interesting throughout, and do what we need them to do so the audience will understand, in the way that we want them to understand, our reference points, at any time in the story. They are going to walk around and say the things that we put in their mouths to say. If the audience cares about your characters, you will engage them and they will follow you for two hours. If your characters are weak, no matter how dynamic the action on the screen is, the audience may follow you, or leave you, but they certainly will not care.

So character will lead you to story—not the other way around. A lot of writers take the opposite approach, and the script reflects it: a situation, pieced together, with no emotional logic running through it. Plot-heavy to justify an idea without the underlying driving force of character that audiences can connect to. We are humans, so we respond to humans: humans within situations, human beings within a story. It is the people, the characters in a story, that we respond to. Their trials, their emotions, their pursuits, the complications in their lives. Our own lives are full of those things, so why not our characters'? Makes sense. We borrow from ourselves and from those around us all the time to write our characters.

For the purpose of learning the craft, which is what we are doing now, we are starting from a blank page, no previously thought-of ideas. I caution you because I know how tempting it can be. However, bringing preconceived ideas with you will only get in your way and impede the learning process. If you have ideas, which no doubt you do, set them aside for now. After you have learned the process, you will have the tools and know what to do with those ideas, how to fulfill them. You can never have too many ideas.

We writers all have different backgrounds. Different educations. Different likes and dislikes and personality traits. We have different family backgrounds. Some of us are outgoing; some of us are quiet. We are different, and out of that difference comes our own individual work. Our own inner being is our best guide, and it is what distinguishes one writer from another. Trust it. Respect it. Train it. Begin to train that inner being to bring out the best writer in you. Later on you will recognize how your own individuality feeds and enriches your work.

The Arbitrary Character

So how do you begin? How do you begin a character sketch? How do you approach the idea of "character"? What do you have to know? What should you think about?

I am asking these questions so you will then know what to ask yourself. What should you be concerned with when contemplating character? What do you write down? Very important.

I mentioned the American novelist Joan Didion in the Introduction, quoting her husband John Dunne, also a novelist, saying, "Making a note as and when it comes to you is the difference between writing and not writing." You are writers. Writers write. Yes, you play in your head. But you write it all down on the page. So what do you have to write down to let your character, the character you are now going to write about, live and breathe and speak and function in his own or her own inimitable way?

Writers I've worked with have often asked me, "Irv, do you do the exercises that you give us?" That's a fair question. My answer is, "Sometimes." Sometimes I do them, depending upon the needs, depending upon the material. And sometimes I don't do them. But always . . . I always do the character exercise.

To introduce you to the specifics of character, I'd like to tell you about something that happened to me a few years ago in Los Angeles. There was a major entertainment-film lawyer who had been kind to me. He liked my work. He had written a few letters for me, drawn up a contract for me, he hadn't charged me the going rate, sometimes he didn't charge me at all, and he'd introduce me to people. He called me one day and said, "Irv, I need you. I need you to help me with a client."

Now the circumstances of that moment were interesting because I had just come back from Seattle where I had been Playwright in Residence at the University of Washington. I took that job for six months because I didn't know anybody in Seattle and I knew that the phone wouldn't be ringing. There was a play I had been working on that I had done my prewriting phase for over a long gestation period and was now ready to write. It was a play that, as a playwright and being Jewish, I knew I had to write one day. It was about the Babi Yar massacre of 34,000 Jewish men, women, and children by the Nazis on the outskirts of Kiev during WWII. I knew that I needed focus and concentration, and my whole work commitment in Seattle was two workshops: an undergraduate Playwriting workshop and a graduate-level Adaptation workshop. So I wrote this play. It was probably one of the hardest things I ever wrote in my life. The day I finished the play, I was overcome with a flood of tears that wouldn't stop.

As I mentioned, I had just got back to New York from Seattle, and this lawyer called from California and said, "Irv, ya gotta help me." He gave me a rough idea of the subject matter and sent me material. The subject matter was Josef Mengele, the infamous SS doctor who performed medical experiments in the death camps in Auschwitz during WWII. I knew I couldn't go there again. The producer had announced it in a full back-page ad in *Variety*. Barbed wire, chimneys, bayonets, babies. Mengele's demonic face, the ugly face of the Holocaust, glaring at us. I responded with an immediate "No."

The idea was like an itch at the back of my mind. There was a job from another producer that was waiting for a green light but looked precarious at best. Like everyone else, I had bills to pay. I also knew that the project my lawyer had called about would end up in the hands of another writer and would likely become "The Holocaust in Disneyland." I thought through how I could approach the subject and called my lawyer in LA and told him I'd do it. "But, I won't do the concentration camps, I won't do the experimentation on babies, I won't do all of that stuff. What I will do is: I'll frame it as an action/adventure. I'll frame it as five people who go to Uruguay, Brazil, wherever, because there is an old man there that they think may be Mengele. They'll bring him out to the World Court . . ." What I would write is the story of why these five people go on this mission to find this old man. All of their logic and all of the emotional and dramatic reasons that compel each of the five characters to go on this mission. We learn of their private journeys as a parallel to the adventure of getting the old man out. The lawyer put the producer in touch with me. He had been told of my conditions. The producer called, and I said, "If you want to do it the way I see it, then I'll do it." And he said, "Oh, yes, yes!" Truth is I could've said, "We'll do it on a basketball court . . ." and he wouldn't have blinked an eye. He was a fellow with money, smitten by movies, but hadn't a clue.

Character Leads to Story

Now, I had nothing to go on. Nothing at all. All I had was five disparate people. Nameless, identity-less people. Five characters in search of a story. So to start, I did the character exercise, the way I always start working on a project. Contractually, I had three months. It took me six weeks of the three months to do all five character sketches, and by the end of that prewriting period, I had the whole story. I had 5, 10, 15 pages for each character. Character took me to story. By the time I had investigated and fleshed out each of the characters to that degree, I was pointed in the direction of story.

I tell you this because it proves out the way that I have worked and what's been successful for me. The other reason, and the relevant one, is that in working on that particular character exercise, a scene materialized that I hadn't really thought of as a scene while doing the exercise. As an exercise, it was a laundry list. The fact is that when I got to the point in writing the script where a particular character comes into the narrative, the character laundry list suggested a scene that was an appropriate and engaging way to get the information out. That is when I decided to use it, and I built around the exercise that was written as a laundry list. The scene effectively illustrates what is necessary in creating a character.

There are five characters that make up the group that go to South America. There's also another man in London who is the Control. He's the person who puts the team together. He's the person who raises the money for the team. Logic says to me that somebody has to pay for five people, all the airfares and living expenses. That is what this man Kaufman does. That is the reason for Kaufman to be in the story. In this particular scene, which takes place in Rome, Kaufman, who is a gentlemanly grandfather type with strength of character, goes to talk to a wealthy young Brazilian playboy in order to ask him for the money to fund the expedition. The scene takes place at a palazzo, at a party that has been arranged in a social setting, so that the meeting can seem casual.

Script Example

Mengele—Kaufman/Guerra—Scene

```
EXT. POLO GROUNDS/ROME -- DAY

A mallet in full swing, hitting a hard wooden ball. Pounding
hoofs. Pull out to take in the excitement of the Polo match
in all of its glory. We see that it is MANRICO GUERRA who has,
very proficiently, hit the ball and now leads the pack towards
the opposing goal. We notice the polo stadium, which is in the
```

heart of Rome, the chic clutch of onlookers. High fashion in
the season. The players thunder up and back, MANRICO GUERRA,
prominent everywhere.

                                                    CUT TO:

GUERRA still in his mud spattered uniform, and a stylish WOLFE
KAUFMAN, ever the man about polo matches, sipping cocktails in
the club area.

                        KAUFMAN
            It *is* a major undertaking and needs . . . major
            financing.

                        GUERRA
            Money . . .?
                (reflectively)
            Why did I have the distinct impression that
            you would ask me to perform some heroic deed?
                (KAUFMAN just stares at him in his
                unflappable way)
            No offence Mr. Kaufman, but . . . I am curious
            . . . Why me? Surely, I have no reputation as
            a philanthropist?

                        KAUFMAN
                (calm, cool, straight at him)
            Manrico Guerra. Home: Sao Paulo , Brazil. 6'3",
            215 lbs, dark hair, brown eyes, 31 years old.
                (GUERRA takes a mock bow, KAUFMAN
                nods his head in return)
            wealthy, athletic, charming to a fault, a
            bit arrogant, with a reputation for acting
            before thinking.
                (GUERRA amused, shrugs)
            Educated at U.C.L.A. Bright, but no scholar.
            Prefers simple concepts, direct action.
            Enthusiastic, always has something to say,
            loudly . . . Is agreeable as long as you agree
            with him.

                        GUERRA
                (enjoying himself)
            What . . . I'm not perfect?

                        KAUFMAN
            Stylish dresser. Latest fashion. A major
            success with the ladies, not ready to settle
            permanently. A taste for the heroic . . . plays
            polo, very well I might add . . .
                (they nod at each other)
            Sky dives, sports car racer, a football star
            without a team. Can't sit still . . . admires
            himself . . . too much.

                        GUERRA
            To ask a man for money . . . shouldn't you be
            . . . flattering him . . .?

                    KAUFMAN
Works in family business . . . when he works.
Coffee . . . vast acreage . . . multi-million
dollar income.

                    GUERRA
                (game over)
I begin to tire.

                    KAUFMAN
Father of Italian descent. Third generation
Brazilian, inherited wealth. Mother . . .

                    GUERRA
                (stands, eyes blazing)
Enough.

                    KAUFMAN
                (calmly, indicating for GUERRA to sit)
Mother . . . Jewish . . .
                (GUERRA angry)
Met and married father when he was an
engineering student in Germany. Her parents
disapproved of her marrying a Catholic,
refused to attend the wedding or to accept her
husband's efforts to get them out of Germany.

They died in Auschwitz . . .

GUERRA slowly sits, not looking at KAUFMAN. A couple pass and
wave at GUERRA, congratulate him on his victory. He smiles and
waves back.

                    KAUFMAN
Has always been a bit afraid of his Jewish
heritage. Has never had any Jewish friends.
Feels Jews were submissive victims,
passive. Things he . . . is . . . so
wholeheartedly . . . NOT. Shall I continue?
                (GUERRA slowly nods and turns toward
                him)
Though he is curious about this side of him
 . . . he has always stayed away from it . . .
one of the only things he consciously . . . fears.

                    GUERRA
How do you know all of . . . this . . .?

                    KAUFMAN
If . . . I am to succeed in what I do . . . I must
know. You are right . . . I was prepared to
flatter . . . charm . . . tell you heart rending
stories . . . There is non time. We have a . . .
pressing engagement.

                    GUERRA
I . . . I . . . will listen.

That's the scene. You also had a dip into Film Form, which we get to later. Look at all that information. Look at what you'll have to know. Not that you'll use everything. But you have to know it. You have to detail it for yourself to possibly use it. In the beginning, you don't know what's going to be important later, so you collect everything. You take everything. I call it the Catch-All Bag. Everything goes in. Later, certain things will bubble to the top as more important than others. Some things you won't use at all. You have to begin to collect that kind of material and, as you proceed through the period of this gathering phase, you to begin to know your material intimately.

Character Bio

So what do you have to know to build a character?

You have to know physically what your characters look like. And don't avoid the obvious. When people say good-looking . . . what does that mean? Elaborate on that. Brown hair, blonde hair, thin face, pretty . . . what? What makes pretty? Perhaps even in this particular moment, in this particular person . . . what makes pretty? You've got to know physically.

You've got to know socially. Does the person have a family? Does the person not have a family? Is the person a loner? How old is the person? What kind of food does he or she like?

What kind of educational background does the person have? Because that is going to affect that person's way of functioning, their activities, their way of speaking.

Did he or she serve in the military? May apply, may not.

You have to know psychologically. Does the person have hang ups? Does the person like people, not like people? We all don't function in the same way, and it is because of all of these intricacies, these nuances.

So socially, psychologically, physically—basically as much as we can determine at this point in our discovery. Understanding that we will fill in hazy spots or blank spots later as we find out more. And it is appropriate to say, "I don't know. At this point, I don't know." At this point, you may not have all the answers to all the questions you ask yourself. But you've got to know and begin with the basics.

So: "character." I want you to choose a character, and don't overthink it—I really mean that. This is not going to be the greatest story ever told. You are learning a craft, not writing a script . . . yet. Make an arbitrary choice. A character. Somebody that you make up or somebody you've known or know. Make a choice and go with it based on what you have just understood. Write what you think is important to know about that character. And, again, I caution you: Avoid all thoughts of story. For purposes of learning the craft of screenwriting, I want you to approach each element of the craft separately as a stand-alone. I promise you: We will get to the script eventually.

Now—and this is important—there is no right way to do this or wrong way to do this. You cannot get this exercise wrong. You do it any way you want to because it is your own investigation, for yourself. Nobody else sees it except you, so it doesn't matter how you write it—but write it. Make your notes. No serious writer goes from a shred of an idea in their head or a fragment of a character they've thought of straight to the page, expecting inspiration to do the work for them at each turn. Reliance on inspiration leads to the "what comes next" approach. A waste of time. To be candid, it is the way an amateur works. You are moving to a different level now.

The character exercise is also an exercise that does not end. You are not going to know everything about this character in your first go. The character evolves as a result of information that you find as you proceed through the other exercises and as your imagination makes connections to the situations and circumstances that emerge. Now, if you ponder the idea of character a little, you quickly realize that all characters are not going to say things in the same way. They won't react in the same way because they don't come out of the same backgrounds. So, did your character go to university? Has he/she a master's degree? If so, the character is not going to say what a person who quit school in the fourth grade says. They may say the same things, but they aren't going to say them in the same way. We have to be aware of that. We do a lot of this stuff subliminally. We don't have to make a big effort to think about a lot of this stuff, but there's some of it that's worth thinking about, that's worth concerning yourself with, worth stopping to ask yourself, "Did I think about that?"

For our purposes now, to understand and start using this most fundamental approach to the craft, I ask you to limit your character to one page of description, tops. Or make a list. Whatever you do, limit it. You've got to know and begin.

Location

As part of this first assignment, you are also going to choose a location. An Indoor Location and an Outdoor Location. This means locations that this character is somehow related to, or involved with for some reason. It can be where he or she lives or whatever you choose. An Outdoor Location and an Indoor Location somehow related to this character, where the character could be found, or passes through, or goes to sit and contemplate. Now, just as in describing the character, in describing the location you won't just say, "a beautiful park." What makes it beautiful? Is it big or is it small? Are there people in it? Is it deserted? Are the benches old wooden benches or sleek modern metal ones? Are there benches at all? So, two locations for you to describe in a couple of sentences, a paragraph at most.

Time Frame

The third part of the exercise is the time frame. And the time frame I am going to suggest you use is "now." We don't need to stretch too much: It's present day, present time. Time—used in this case as a different reference point, when we talk about time frame in a story—not only means present day, it can also mean identifying the season, as it may have an application: Summer, Winter, Spring, or Fall. It can mean knowing the month because people function differently in the month of May than they do in December. So we might be interested in the month. We might be interested in the day of the week because people function differently on Friday than they do on Monday morning. And the hour of the day, whether it is dawn or dusk or twilight or whatever, because, again, it has a bearing on the way people function. Later you'll see that time has yet a different use in the context of Film Form. Time is always designated in Film Form, for multiple reasons, but suffice to say for now, so that the writer can't get lost in his or her own time frame as it applies to the story, that time is an interesting and very useful part of telling a screen story. Time allows for color, for mood, for tension. Time has multiple implications and it is essential that we begin to be aware of the time factor in our stories.

Personal History

Give me a personal reason why this particular character is in this location. A one- or two-line description. For example: The character is in this Italian town to look at the frescos, or to study the frescos . . . or to go to this little chapel up in the hills where they have this special mass . . . or whatever the reason is that your imagination suggests. Make a choice. Pick one out of the air and write it. That applies to all these exercises. Don't concern yourself with how or if they connect; it will get you in a mess and suggest story, and then you get caught up in trying to justify. Avoid going to story.

Student Exercise Examples

The students' work that I have included in this book all come out of my classes in Spoleto, Italy, or New York, or from one-on-one tutorials with students from all over the world. Let's look at some of them to see how my instructions have translated into their first exercise. They are for clarification and to help while doing your own exercises. Now as you recall—I said it earlier—it doesn't matter how you do the exercise, in what form, or in what order.

So let's start with Mark's example.

Time Frame: October 17, 2006. 9am as the convent rings its first bell of the day inside the walls.

Outside Location: Outside the main gate of the Convent St Angelo in Spoleto.

Inside Location: The main courtyard and gardens

Character: Paolo D'Amari, age 83, lives in an elder care facility outside of Rome.

Marital Status: Widower, married to Stella Farini (from old Spoleto family) for 62 years, but she is now 6 months deceased.

Children: Two sons, one is 59 one residing in Philadelphia another is 57 residing in NY.

Heritage: Both parents from Perugia.

Education: Only through the 7th grade.

Military: Served under Mussolini—not proud of it.

Health (physical and/or emotional): Frail, missing his wife terribly, subject to panic attacks and night upon night of fitful sleep, depression in general, facing his mortality.

Physical appearance: Medium height, what's left of a barrel chest, otherwise lean, bald, wise eyes, a bit hunched but still showing a ruddiness and complexion implying a guarded vitality.

Background: Paolo was once head grounds keeper at the Villa Monte Vista. Very proud of his design and maintenance of the gardens. Fell in love with Stella at the Villa and eventually eloped with her, causing a schism in her family and eventual ostracism, but she was never fully cut off from inheriting her portion of the estate. Although she and Paolo presumed so.

While working and living modestly at the Villa Paolo invented an irrigation system, that he eventually sold the patent for to a manufacturer in Milan, allowing him enough money to run away with Stella and to marry her. He went on to invent several other things of merit but not to much avail . . .

Good. That's a beginning. A real taste, and that's what we want at this moment. A taste particular enough to whet our, the writer's, appetite to want to find out more. This is an exercise for our own use. To work from as a jumping off point.

Adjustments: What Mark has designated as his Indoor Location is, from the perspective of writing for film, an outdoor location. An Indoor Location is basically a space with walls and a roof. It is a physical designation of space not from a narrative point of view. The second issue is that he does not give us a Personal History. We don't have any idea why his character is at the convent. Maybe Mark just doesn't know yet, and that is okay. If it is not something simple, it is better to say "I don't know" than to start building a story in your head as Mark has begun to do.

Now be prepared that as we dig further, we may find contradictory material, so the adjustment will be to change what we originally had. We may find we need our character to be short rather than tall. Slim rather than stocky. In his 40s instead of in his 20s. You must stay open to your material all the time. As I said earlier, this exercise doesn't end, which means that as we go through the other exercises, we will find and add more information about the character.

Writing is an organic process. Nothing is written in stone. For the purpose of learning the process, some limitations must apply, but even within those limitations we must always leave room for change. I'll be more specific on the subject of change as we move forward. You will see that it all depends on where the character is going and what we need to say in our stories. It is, as we proceed, what we need the character to do and say that allows us to make choices about what to keep and what not to keep. So you will add to your character as we go. At this point, you are not responsible for story. You need to be firm about that. It is very tempting, and I've had students come in and proudly announce, "I did my character exercise and I have my whole story." Fight that impulse. You will be locking in too early.

All right, let's continue and look at just Time Frame and Location in Sue's exercise.

Indoor Location: Il Doumo. La Duomo. Not sure. In front of the candles lit by supplicants . . . there's a small table, very old fashioned with metal candle cups and a large box with white candles with a collection box strategically placed to the right of it. The area around the table is dimly lit smooth gray stone with a fresco of St Francis of Assisi or some such saint, arms out stretched in Welcome.

Outdoor Location: The Aqueduct off the jogging path, this old Roman stone structure spans a huge shrub-filled chasm, contemporary looking metallic mirrored sculptures hang in silent juxtapositions, swinging gently in the wind.

Time: Present day, early on a quiet Monday in April, spring flowers dot the hillsides on either side of the Aqueduct.

Good. Another taste. Two adjustments. As Sue finds her story, she will have to look up in an Italian dictionary if it is La Duomo or Il Duomo. It seems like a minor point, but it's worth noting that accuracy is important. Not fact but accuracy. Fact is important when making documentaries but not in narrative film. Second adjustment. Sue refers to the Aqueduct as "a large Roman structure." What is its shape? Are the sculptures hanging from poles on either end of the aqueduct? When we do Location, it is important to think of it in terms of a character. We think in terms of particularizing, just as we do a character. Remember, it can't be in your head because you may forget the details that made it notable when you actually sit down to write your script. The same adjustment applies to Sue's Indoor location, "a typical Italian church." Are there pews or benches? Are they old? What's the wood look like? What color are the walls? Are they peeling or freshly painted? The high ceiling—what is the lighting like? We want to know what makes that location, if anything, unusual, surprising.

It is also acceptable to deal with location in generalities. "The interior of an Italian church." What you, the writer, are then saying is, "Set Designer, I leave it to you." If there is something unusual about it, some quality, some aspect of that church that you want to draw out, if it is something significant, you put it in. You, the writer, are creating a sense of place that is particular to the story you want to tell so that the reader of the script—the director, let's say—begins to enter the moment that is about to take place in the location you design. When we get to the chapter on Film Form you will see there are also certain specifics that must be included on the page.

Ok, so now let's look at what Carmen did. Interesting; she gave it a title. She calls it "Etude In Coo." It's good to start with a working title as long as you're not locking yourself into a story. Something simple that you might change six times before choosing one title at the end.

Character: Pancredi, a pigeon—is of medium size, slightly plump with scruffy gray feathers and beady eyes that wink. He is middle aged, resourceful and independent. He has always been the philosopher and the socially conscious one in any group. Pancredi was nurtured under the town clock in the Piazza del Mercato. His mother and five siblings flew away when he was eight weeks old never to be seen again. He is a bachelor bird who knows all the towns of Umbria well. He has a slightly gravely voice with a hint of mischief in it. He lives with a group of other pigeons, about five in all at any given time, all male. The pigeons are always talking and grumbling and making a racket especially in the morning and late afternoon.

Personal History: Pancredi lives on a street in the centro storico section of Spoleto.

Outdoor Location: Pancredi's home is on a ledge on the Via Brignone above a blinking traffic light on the shady side of the street. The building is an unremarkable seventeenth century structure four stories high. The ledge is on the second floor front window, the windows on that floor are always closed, it appears that no one lives there. The outside wall of the building is typically distempered and in a state of decline. Around the ledge the outer layers of plaster and cement have fallen away leaving the exposed skeletal stones. On either side of the ledge various stones have fallen out leaving perfect apartments for the five feathered bon vivants.

Indoor Location: I don't have one yet.

Time: It is about 7am, August in Spoleto.

Good enough exercise. I am intrigued . . . beginnings of a good character. And she says she doesn't have an indoor location yet. That's okay; granted, she does have a problem since a pigeon is not likely to be indoors. I accept hers as a beginning attempt. No doubt as the story reveals itself, she will find it will take her indoors at some point. So, you see, even with animation, in this case a pigeon, you do the same kind of background for the character, you do the same kind of serious designation of location and time frame; the same approach is necessary.

The next example is from Johanne from Denmark, who did a one-on-one tutorial with me. She had received her degree in film studies but, as is frequently the case, the courses only covered the creative process in generalities. She now wanted to learn specifically about how to write a screenplay.

Who: A 76 year old man, born and raised in Britain. He has grey wavy shoulder long hair that are neatly combed. He has high cheekbones that are highlighted with a peachy blush. His deep sunken brown eyes are enhanced with fake eyelashes and a shiny purple eyeshadow. His lips are always painted with a light pink lipstick and a clear gloss that makes them seem fuller. The skin on his face is wrinkled but velvet soft. He loves wearing woolen turtleneck sweaters, pencil skirts and shiny black loafers. He is a twin but grew up as an only child because his brother died during childbirth. His father owned a printing house in London and his mum was a housewife and a private vocal coach. He got his first kiss from a girl called Iris when he was 9 years old. 12 years later he married her and they got one son that he hasn't seen in years. He has a german shepherd and lives in New York City. He loves drinking a bitter with his breakfast and listening to Édith Piaf.

Indoor: A tiny cinema. The hallway has a checkered black and white floor, white walls that have turned yellow over the years decorated with ornamented golden picture frames with movieposters—old and new. In the front there is a small ticket booth operated by a lazy teenager who is most likely the daughter of the owner. The cinema has two auditoriums that are both named after former Hollywood stars. Our character prefers the smallest one that seats only 40 people. Every Wednesday afternoon he sinks into one of the red velvet chair with slack springs and flat padding to review movie classics.

Outdoor: A cemetery with beautiful pink cherry trees that have started to wither. Gravel walkways separate and intersect in an uneven pattern. Dogs are allowed if on a leash. There are tombstones in any shape and size. Some burial sites are decorated with fresh flowers and picture frames. Others are poorly kept and seem like they haven not had visitors in years. The sound of kids playing in a nearby schoolyard fills the air with laughter and joy. Our character goes there from time to time to visit someone that he loved very much.

Time: A Sunday in May at 10.30 am

Good. So the first seeds of thinking like a screenwriter have been planted. Now, at this juncture students often ask, "Irv, are we married to this character?" The answer is "No . . . up until the character starts to speak, and then, for the purposes of learning the process, you are committed." That is among the few limitations I mentioned earlier that I will be applying to the work we do together.

One last instruction before we move on: Do not give your work to any-one else to read. Do not look for validation; you will only get confused. It is important to understand that the work at this stage is between you and you. Others, though well meaning, will all have something to say and you will find yourself going down a different path every time you turn around.

Writing for film, and I mean feature film (not documentary), requires a very different way of thinking than writing a novel or an essay or a technical business report or a short story. Being a writer is a solitary profession and it is important that you begin to trust yourself. That you begin to hear yourself. That you develop a thread of your own logic in your own work.

So we are beginning the process of screenwriting with Character.

This is a good place to repeat: Do not overthink this exercise. This is the beginning. Make a choice about your character, the location, and the time frame. Why he or she is there. A character of your own choosing and why is that character here: that's all we want to know.

Exercise #1—Character, Location, Time Frame

Character

1. Choose an arbitrary character, one you have not thought about or worked on before.
2. Write what you think would be important to know about the charac-ter. Think in terms of physical, psychological, social, family, education, among the characteristics. It is a first impression, a shorthand mini bio of the character.

Pre-History

Two or three lines of why this particular character is in this location.

Location

Describe an indoor and an outdoor location.

Time Frame

Delineate the time frame the character is in these locations.

Write the exercise any way you want to. You cannot get it wrong. It is the beginning of your research for *yourself*. It is also an exercise that does not end. As you find out more about the character in the following exer-cises, you will add to your character's bio. This exercise is all you need to think about at this point. You are learning a craft, a process. Which is to say: AVOID jumping to story!

Enjoy yourself.

TWO

Character Out
Loud—Dialogue

We've begun our gradual discovery of the process with the identification of character. We've made our first choices. As a writer, you will be making choices all the time. Very important to let that start settling in to your understanding of what being a writer is. So, we have a character and we've put that character into an outdoor and an indoor location. The locations relate to this character in some way. The person walks by them, or goes inside them, or is involved with them in some peripheral way or important way. And we've designated a time frame. It takes place sometime in recent times in those two locations. We were not thinking about *what* takes place or *why* it takes place.

Now what we are going to do is allow this character, that we have chosen, that we have begun to have a feel for, to speak in his or her own inimitable voice. This brings us to examine what dialogue means specifically in terms of Film. Many would-be screenwriters are drawn to writing for film because they have a good ear. They have a feel for what people say and can make friends laugh. That is not a bad thing, as long as you realize, and you will as we move further into the process, that dialogue is only a part of your responsibility and that having a good ear might mean only being able to mimic what people say and how they say it. First, be aware that what we are writing will not be experienced internally; it will be out loud. When you read novels or short stories or journals, you are filtering it passively through the mechanism of your mind. You are responding to it, deciphering what it means, by filtering words on a page mentally. We, as screenwriters and playwrights, have different responsibilities; we are writing to be heard—out loud, in the moment, for an audience to react to immediately in the way that we want them to, within a continuous narrative. The tonality, the inflection—we write dialogue that does not depend on lengthy descriptions and internal explorations of characters, as a novel does. You can put a book down. With a movie, you are there from beginning to end in one sitting. Big difference.

So what is dialogue in film?

Producers and directors talk about wanting real dialogue. But they don't mean real. What they mean is the illusion of the way people speak. Made-up dialogue that sounds real. If you were to record real dialogue as you hear it in normal conversation, most of it would be boring. What we do as screenwriters is alter real dialogue, extracting the essence. We engage our audience in the moment so they follow us for two hours. And by the word 'essence' I don't mean dots and dashes; I mean full expressions but without the boring parts of 'real' or 'normal' dialogue. This is then further nuanced by the fact that people speak in different ways, depending on many variables. Because of the peculiarities of background. Because of the specifics of education. Because of social circumstances. Because of all those things that require one character to say one thing and another character to say the same things but in a different way. It's logical. They may say the same thing but the way they say it will be different. And we have to write our dialogue in character, the particular way our characters would say whatever it is they are going to say. Take, for example, a weary man who wants his wife to agree to stop so they can sit down and eat something. A worldly traveler would say it one way and a laborer working in the fields would say it in a very different way.

Sources of Dialogue

Now, even though I have said normal dialogue is boring, one of the best sources of dialogue is normal conversation. People do say the most extraordinary things all the time and nobody hears the gems. We are geared to listen, but we *hear* only fragments of information because we are already thinking in terms of how we're going to respond, how we are going to answer.

I was on a cafeteria line in upstate New York once. I am standing online . . . long line, with my plate, and I'm waiting. There's a line up of people—nice people—and lots of individual tables. A little kid is running around, between people's legs, stepping on people's shoes, and people are nice, saying, "Oh isn't he cute?" Not cute . . . major pain! And everybody is trying to be nice about it. I'm standing there watching this and at a table close to the line there is a young woman, an attractive woman, dressed nicely, she's staring at some unseen crack in the ceiling. It's the kid's mother. Opposite her is the kid's grandmother. Watching the kid. The grandmother's so angry that smoke is coming out of her ears. You can see her teeth clenching. The kid runs by. Finally, the grandmother grabs the kid, shakes the kid and says: "Breathe in, breathe out . . . you're just like your father . . . breathe in, breathe out." Now what the hell does that mean? I am sure nobody else on the line heard. I grabbed my spiral notebook, wrote it down. Extraordinary way of expressing oneself. Not thought out, just blurted out. You couldn't make that up. Amazing. A tasty morsel to save and use one day.

Another moment: I was in the elevator of my building with a neighbor and her young son. The kid was a delicious, cocky five year old. The mother and I were talking about them considering moving out of New York; the kid would have a yard to play in and all that. So I looked down at the kid and asked, "What do you think?" He said, "My mother is a city mouse, my father is a country mouse, and I am a political mouse." A five-year-old! I took out my notebook. What a response. Tickled me to no end.

What I am suggesting is you've got to listen. Keep your antenna up. If what you hear or see does not pertain to the story you are working on now . . . save it for later. I've done that a lot because one of the things we do as writers is we borrow from ourselves. We thought we were going to use something in one particular story but we didn't, and now we find it fits perfectly into this other story we are writing. We also borrow from our imagined selves. We have all been in situations where we are confronted with an issue or a concern or some dramatic moment or situation, and we come out of it and shortly after we say, "God . . . why didn't I say . . . I could've said . . . I should've said . . . I might've said . . ."

Monologue

Monologue/Aria: Expression of Character/Personality

In the discussion of dialogue, I want first to consider the monologue. What do people say? One person: How does that person, your character, express himself or herself? To give you a good sense, here are some examples. This first one is a scene from my script *High Octane*, which is a story about an oil shortage. Two guys, a white guy named Matt and a black guy named Connor, are put together by an oil company to share the expense of a gas station. They are business partners, not friends; in fact, they don't really like each other. Connor is driving Matt home, and this is the lead-in to the monologue.

Script Examples

```
INT. CAR - LATE AFTERNOON

Matt stares ahead. Conner drives.

                    MATT
        I . . . I said dumb things.

                    CONNER
        Me too. You right I got big mouth. Always did.
                    MATT
        You ah . . . I ah . . . Thanks for . . .
        (Conner nods and the men awkwardly try to
        apologize to each other. It is a difficult but
        feeling moment in its awkwardness.)
```

                              CONNER
                    (As they pass some kids playing
                    basketball in a school yard.)
          Way back . . . I was a basketball
          player . . . nothin' big . . . High
          School . . . but we were real good.
          Won everythin' in sight . . . City
          champs . . . Everybody cheerin'
          us . . . little celebrities . . .
                    (laughs)
          Kids . . . jus' kids . . .
                    (shrugs)
          These guys . . . come hangin' aroun' knowed 'em
          from the street . . . bad guys . . . who the Hell
          knew the difference . . . say we don' have to
          lose . . . we win . . . you dig . . . but by
          points . . . less points . . . We
          win . . . make a few bucks too . . . Hey,
          fine threads . . . wine . . . lil' ol' gels
          that were everywhere. We all happy. It
          was somethin'. For one shiny mo . . . we
          were, "Somebody" . . . anythin' . . .
          everythin' . . . was possible . . . then . . .
          then . . . the music stopped . . . sky fell in
          on our heads . . . T.V., papers full of it. We
          dumpers . . . Un- American . . . baddest dudes ever
          born . . . Basketball never the same again . . .
          What could you believe in . . .? Make lil'
          kids cry. Felt bad . . . kicked off the
          team . . . outta school . . . no college . . . no
          future . . . A couple bucks . . . an' we
          didn't lose . . . So I took a hit . . . a
          snort . . . an' another . . . Who the Hell
          cared what happened?

INT.CAR - LATE AFTERNOON

The car parked by the curb. Conner starting into his memory.
Matt watches him intently.

                              CONNER
          . . . Skeets, this little inch of a guy . . .
          mighty mite 'fore little men were "in". . .
          ran around, through people and funny ooooo
          weeeeee . . . My man. . .ran together, hit
          the bads together, he laughin' sayin' it
          all gone soon . . . outta sight . . . outta . . .
          but nobody forget . . . not me. . .not
          him . . . then Skeets up an' OD'd dead,
          gone. . .nothin' . . .
                    (quiet)
          I knowed . . . he died of a broken heart . . .
          took our dreams away. Been hard, man . . .
          real hard yo climb out . . . feel somethin'
          for myself again. . .I go home to my wife 'n

```
                        kids. . . Jimmy, Ellen. . .good kids . . . play
                        with 'em . . . homework . . . like watchin' 'em
                        . . . I . . . I not so angry anymore . . . an'
                        now . . . maybe I could . . . maybe we . . . you
                        an' me . . . could . . . we could try . . .


INT. BAR - LATE AFTERNOON

Matt and Conner sitting in a booth in a bar having beer.

                                  MATT
                        . . . an' she works . . . as an editor, does it
                        at home . . . propped up in bed . . . or at the
                        kitchen table . . . She's good . . . in demand.
                        Does her share.
                                  (takes deep breath)
                        Didn't have any kids . . . always so
                        much we wanted to do. There was time you
                        know . . . time  . . . Not . . . huh . . .
                                  (shrugs)
                        the way she battles the stairs . . . half an hour
                        to get up two flights of stairs . . . twice a day . . .
                        "her stairs" she says . . .
                                  (shakes his head)
                        getting worse . . . harder . . . she falls . . . won't
                        give in . . . won't quit . . . day in, day
                        out . . . insists on cooking . . . shopping . . .
                        Maintenance she calls it . . . drags herself . . .
                        worries about me . . . my little problems . . . the
                        station . . . the gas line . . . the bullshit . . .
                                  (Conner nods)
                        Sometimes . . . I just feel like going . . .
                        going . . . I don't know where . . . just
                        going . . . I think . . . what the Hell I need
                        it for . . . fighting for every inch, every breath
                        . . . sickness . . . Paco's nuts but I know
                        what he feels . . . inside like he wants
                        somethin' soft . . . for once . . . soft . . .
                        an', an'. . . I just go.
                                  (Conner nods in recognition)
```

Now that's not only one monologue—and I like to call them arias—that's two arias back to back. On the screen that will hold because the rhythms are good and the expression of their individuality is strong enough. The character identification is clear enough, the dramatic moment is solid enough that it will hold. Two speeches back to back and the audience will listen.

Here is another one from a script I wrote called *The Elephant Is Well*. It's not about a sick elephant. It's about five Italian men in the 1980s who live in the Little Italy section of New York City. None of the five have done anything significant in their lives. It's about a misunderstanding between one of those men, Vittorio, and a 45-year-old Jewish dentist, Stuart. Later in the film he is called "Stu da dentis" because they think he's a criminal.

Stuart is an amateur photographer and one day he is walking around in Little Italy and he takes a picture of Vittorio, who has a great face. Stuart submits it to a magazine contest and the prize is that they print the picture. However, if it is a portrait the submission requires a release form signed by the subject. So Stuart takes a 4×5 photo and goes down to Little Italy and tries to find the old man. Now, if you go down to Little Italy with a 4×5 photo and you start showing people a picture of someone, what is the response going to be? Nobody knows him. Nobody has ever seen him. They have no idea who it could be. This escalates because the police are now looking for Vittorio. Which escalates into the FBI looking for Vittorio. A big fiasco of a scene where everybody gets involved, the police, the FBI, the television studios, everybody. Finally, Stu and Vittorio, still not aware of the eruption of WWIII end up on the Staten Island Ferry together and that's where this speech takes place. This is Vittorio's speech. . . .

EXT. OPEN WATER - STATUE OF LIBERTY - NIGHT STATUE OF LIBERTY

her torch electrically lit, her crown sparkling . . . her presence glowing in the blackness of the night.

> VITTORIO (V.O.)
> Come . . . come . . . she say "We wanna you come be happy . . ."

                                                        CUT TO:

EXT. STATEN ISLAND FERRY - NIGHT

VITTORIO & STU on the rail of the Staten Island Ferry just passing the Statue of Liberty.

> VITTORIO
> . . . and we come . . . why not? An you know somethin', Mista' . . . we gotta roof . . . we gotta work . . . we gotta full belly . . . we gotta respec . . . (he shrugs) Menaggia . . . okay . . . okay . . . I don' ask for no medal. . . jus. . . jus. . . (turns all his anger pouring out) Fifty years collec garbage. . . clean a da street. . . i's awrigh. . . I don owe nobody notin . . . one day dey give me a party . . . So long Vito . . . You a good guy, Vito . . . arrivederci . . . somebody pass a law I too ole . . . today you needa college to collec crap . . . Drop dead Vittorio.

He stares out into the night. STU starts to say something. Thinks better of it. Quiet. We still see the Statue of Liberty in the background.

                    VITTORIO
            (starts to laugh . . . remembering)
Ha . . . you shoulda seen them . . . shiny
uniforms . . . red and green. . .and a
big colored plume sticking up from their
hats . . . I Busuglieri . . .
            (imitates blowing a horn . . . waving
it) I used to follow dem . . . all aroun da
square in da middle o town . . .
            (laughs)
That square was da whole town. On one
side . . . da mountain . . . an da castle . . .
ahh . . . to sit in da cafe . . . talk
friendly . . . drink a little espresso . . .
spend time with your people. The women
sunning themselves in the doorways . . . the
unmarried ones seated with their backs to da
streets. We live inna village thousand years..
poor..sure . . . but alive. Now my nephews'
kid . . . wans to go to da moon. . .
            (turns to Stu sadly)
Who are dey? I don understan what they say. I
don' know wha they mean. Wha is in da hearts
. . . Drop dead, Vito . . . Maybe itsa me on da
moon. What kinda name is Stu da Dentis?

                    STU
I'm a dentist.

                    VITTORIO
No . . . you a fer real dentis?

STU nods apologetically. VITTORIO looks around, then confidentially
imparting the most intimate of secrets.

                    VITTORIO
I gotta teet . . . But . . . I canna read wit
dem . . .

Expression of exasperation. STU completely confused.

                    VITTORIO
I comma 'ome at nighta. We eat . . . no talk.
Marie got nothin to say . . . an the kids
blastin on the TV, who can hear? I sit down to
read da paper . . . an in a few minutes . . . I
fall asleep . . . me head . . .
            (tilts his head down)
an da teet . . .

Makes a gesture indicating the teeth popping out . . . to
appropriate noise he makes with his lips.

                        STU
            (he understands) You can't read with them . . .
                                            CUT TO:

INT. DENTIST'S OFFICE - NIGHT STU'S OFFICE

VITTORIO in the chair, the white gown over him. His mouth wide
open and STU talking as he works over him . . .

                        STU
            . . . I'm not complaining . . . I don't want you
            to think that I'm complaining.

Changes instruments. Back into his mouth.

                        STU
            What have I got to complain about? I got two
            daughters . . . nice kids. One thinks I'm
            archaic . . . to the other I'm just
            superfluous . . . hold still.

He adjust the treatment light and changes instruments again.

                        STU
            I've got everything a man could . . . so why
            should I complain . . .

Back into his mouth as VITTORIO shakes his head.

                        STU
            The girls think I'm crass. Marlyn
            says . . . I'm not original . . . not
            spontaneous . . . not romantic. All
            I think about is work . . . the house . . .
            the two cars . . . the places by the ocean.
            Samantha's college, complete with
            dorm mates . . . Debbie's commune . . .
            Listen . . . my father couldn't carry a load
            like that. I'm blessed.
            (holding Vittorio's jaw in place) Hold still . . .
            your own portable bill payer, that's what I am.
            Where's my inner meaning? Romance?
            (bends closer to Vittorio's ear) I've never told
            anyone . . . my wife . . . she's a clothes junkie.
            Buy . . . buy . . . buy . . . bargain
            basements . . . thrift shops . . . bazaars. She
            believes in quantity at low cost. Then every
            morning, she delicately steps nude onto the
            scale for the ritual, "weighing in."
            (covers his eyes, groans)
            Oh my God . . . one quarter of a pound. "I have
            nothing to wear." And we're off on a Korean

```
rice and avocado diet, with optional fast days
. . . Hey listen to me . . . it's nothing . . .
Who can fault her for trying to find herself if
she thinks she's lost . . . I wouldn't want you
to think . . .
        (sadly)
it's just that sometimes the fallout . . .
(shakes head wearily)
```

One man, one speech . . . one musical sound incorporating what I knew about his background into the way he expressed himself in one speech. I am concerned with the rhythms of that character, his particular music. What he sounds like. I am talking about a personal expression in dialogue that really gives us, if we can, the essence of who this character is. And, at the bottom of it all what we are really after, what we are really concerned about is the emotion. Emotion. If you can't identify the emotion at the core of the material, you won't have a story of any value. In the back of our minds is always, "What's going on here emotionally?" By emotion I don't mean a display of emotion. What is the emotional undercurrent? You want to avoid sentimentality. So emotionally as well as pictorially, actively, dramatically, etc. What is the emotion underpinning this scene, this story?

Student Exercise Examples

Here is an example written almost as one would a novel. Nur is reaching for a character and a moment driven by some emotional motivation.

Nur

Exercise 2

PREHISTORY

```
A month ago in the early morning, one Friday, Seljuk takes a walk
around his neighborhood in Amman. The streets are quiet. Everyone's
sleeping on this weekend holiday. He walks through gravel roads and
side streets, and as he's looking around he spots the remains of a
building, which probably fell in the 1920 quake. He had always seen
it but never really noticed it. Today he goes in and looks around.
Nothing in there, empty and full of collapsed rock. As he turns to
leave, a magnificent stone catches his attention. He walks up to it.
It has text in Turkish and another language, which he can't figure
out. The 15th century Turkish text is written by Barbarossa, the
legendary corsair of the Ottoman Empire who controlled all of the
North African and Mediterranean area and sea trade. But even a Turk
like Seljuk cannot decipher the Turkish text because it is written
in ancient Turkish script. Is it information that he's passing
```

on? This is what he has been looking for, for years, in fact what governments have been looking for. And now he finds it in the most obvious and unlikely place. The stone looks like it is part of the building. It's quite large, smooth, and oval shaped with a flat bottom. The next day he drives his car to the location and brings his gardener to help him steal it back to his house at the Dead Sea where he locks it away in a room. But as small cities have eyes his moving the stone drew the attention of higher authorities who are now after him for something, they do not yet know what. Seljuk does not want to give the stone to authorities without first finding out what the stone says. But in order to keep the stone, he has to commit a crime. He is going through a crisis and has reached the limit of his capacities.

* * *

OCTOBER, EARLY EVENING, TUESDAY

Seljuk pours himself yet another glass of whiskey and unlocks the bedroom door for the third time today. He sets eyes on the stone and takes a huge gulp of his drink. He closes his eyes tight, savoring the deliciously strong flavor and the zing it gives him. He stares at the rock for a while as he takes a few more gulps. Then he slams his glass down on the night table and walks right up to the painting. Grabs it angrily with both hands.

Rabab, speak to me . . . tell me what I need to know. (He says this with urgency in his voice and while shaking the painting, then he hangs it up and takes another swig of whiskey).

You are the great, great, great granddaughter of Barbarossa, you must know! . . . What are you hiding from me? (His voice getting louder. He takes another sip of whiskey and then start biting his nails, one by one, till they are red with blood. He hates feeling weak, but since no one is looking, he lets himself go.)

You women destroy my life. 1 am 53 and lost everything. My daughter ran away, my other daughter will do anything to get the stone, my wife stopped talking to me and now she is bedridden with terminal illness. (He bites his nails even more vigorously. As he takes another big gulp he lets out a sob. He clenches his fist). And now you!

What shall I do? . . . Commit a crime? Is the text on the stone worth it? (He takes the last gulp of whiskey and throws the ice across the room.)

Okay, that's good. We get a good feeling for Seljuk. Nur came with an idea she wanted to write about. I suggest working with a character without any notion of an idea. At this early stage it works against you to have a preconceived idea of story. Why? Because you find yourself fitting your exercise to your story instead of writing the exercise as an unfettered example of, in this case, a monologue. It works as a monologue, but she will have trouble as we move along in the process disengaging from story in order to understand and learn the process. But fine. I accept. And as it turned out, she did very well.

Now in this next example, Johanne had worked on film before, so she had some knowledge of form. My notes on her pages are mostly about the 'directions.' And in the next chapter, we will go into more detail on the whole subject of Film Form.

Screenwriting workshop fall 2014   *Johanne* – Exercise 2: Dialogue

Prehistory:

Our character let's call him Archie, short for Archibald, is at the funny little movie theatre described in exercise 1. He is about to buy a ticket from the lazy teenager operating the ticketbooth. She is wearing a white T-shirt with the words "To be, or not to be…" written in bold red letters across her chest. It reminds our character of a night from his youth where he went to see a Shakespeare play in a West End Theatre with a couple of friends from University.

ARCHIE

(With a clear, deep voice and a British accent) ~~that bear the mark of Archie's many years living in America~~

"To be, or not to be, that is the question"

The lazy teenager looks up from the ~~japanese manga she is reading~~ *both mangas is* No recognition. Archie makes a little nod towards her shirt. She follows Archie's gaze and looks back at him ~~with a~~ ~~look saying "and?"~~

~~ARCHIE~~ *archie* Fill the pause)

(In the same tone as before but ~~with~~ more enthusiasm ~~this time~~)

"Whether 'tis Nobler in the mind to suffer The Slings and Arrows of outrageous Fortune (a tiny pause) Or to take Arms against a Sea of troubles -"

The girl stares at Archie still uncomprehending.

ARCHIE
(In a quizzical tone)
Hamlet? Shakespeare? Surely you must know William Shakespeare..
The greatest writer of all times, he wrote Romeo and Juliet, you know that one…tragic lovestory they both die in the end… they.. they even made a movie…with DiCaprio and that beautiful blonde girl, what's her name again, Carrie…Cailee

Screenwriting workshop fall 2014   Exercise 2: Dialogue

~~Archie is~~ looking at the girl for help ~~remembering the name and realizes that he lost her more than one breath ago)~~

ARCHIE
(Waving his hand in the air)
Nah forget it...the girls' name, not Shakespeare (raising his eyebrows ~~as he says it~~)... you should look him up on that high-tech phone of yours that you play with all day.....It's spelled S-H-A-K-E-S-P-E-A-R-E... (leaning towards the counter as if he wants to make sure she gets the spelling right)
~~(Pause)~~ *Fill the Pause*
You know I wasn't much older than you when I saw a Shakespeare play for the first time...A Midsummer night's dream...me and my study mates... thought we'd skip class... word was that this fine young woman was playing Helena...turned out I knew this girl from... we were just kids when we first...nah where I am getting at, you don't wanna know all this...

[Archie sighs ~~then remembers what his errand was~~

Anyway...what's showing today my dear?

You see from my notes that Johanne needs to focus her directions. And she needs to put them in parentheses. She also calls for a 'pause.' I say: Fill the pause. I would suggest "(he watches her intently)" or something like that. So in Archie we have an altogether different character, a different tone from the others. We get an idea of who Archie is from what he sounds like. Not just what he says but how he says it.

Here's one from Sabina. Sabina had taken a class from me before and was familiar with Film Form, which we go into in the next chapter.

```
Sabina
New York, July 2010

DIALOGUE EXERCISE

Main character, Cass, witnesses a quarrel between his female
roommate and her daughter, 11 years old, in their apartment.
Mother is being a little rough on daughter, because she would
rather paint than do homework. The daughter rushes out of
the door, towards the exterior location of the beach and Cass
follows her. She stops at the water's edge and picks up pebbles
to throw them in the water. Cass quietly walks down to stand
next to her then starts throwing rocks in the water as well.
```

CASS
(hesitant)

You know, you're gonna hate me for saying this, but she's
right . . . Daughter looks up, slightly defensive.
CASS (CONT'D)

But, only partly . . . There has to be room for you to paint,
of course. Cass picks up a piece of driftwood in the surf and
gives it to daughter.
CASS (CONT'D)

You can use this . . . *After* your homework is done . . .
Listen, I know how easy it is to get caught up. It builds up,
it's hard to restrain. It keeps coming at you. But sometimes
you have to put it in a box on a shelf and take it down for
later use. Don't be afraid that it will disappear. You have
nothing to worry about, your creativity is not going away.
Ever. The box will stay on the shelf and you can take it down
and put it back up as much as you want, but it won't magically
disappear by itself. Trust me on this one. I've wasted so
much time being scared that I would all of a sudden stop
creating, so whenever I was inspired to do something I would
throw myself at it frantically, forgetting everything else.
I wanted to quit school, work, friends, just so that I could
focus on dragging as much out of my creative bout as possible.
And sometimes I did. I've lost good friends because if this, I
even got fired as a paper boy when I was a teenager, because I
was at home writing what I thought would definitely be my first
record.
(sighs)

My parents didn't know what was going on, because I didn't
tell them. Eventually, I decided to stop biding and just
be who I wanted to be and do what I wanted to do, show
them what I was doing. And it came off a bit dramatic. But
they misunderstood. They just thought I was developing
erratic behaviour, and instead of confronting me, they
assumed . . . things . . . and eventually had me admitted to a
mental institution.

Daughter takes it, all in, not defensive anymore, but attentive.

CASS (CONT'D)

You are actually in a good position, you know. Your mother
is very supportive and genuinely interested in what you
do, and so am I. But you have to find a way to fit into
the world in your own way. And that's not by ditching
responsibilities or school. You have a lot to learn still,
and it sucks.

Cass gestures with his head for them to go back to the house
and he puts an arm around daughter as they walk.

His monologue is the expression of a reasonable person but stems from experiences of his own so we get some idea of who he is. What I am concerned with is the sound of the character. So Cass is a reasonable fellow.

Character out loud: What is the character's individual sound? How does that character express himself or herself? Is he funny? Is she sarcastic? Is he monosyllabic? Is she educated? Is she a foreigner with a marked accent? Is he angry? How does the character sound when angry?

The Character's Own Sweet Song

I like to call monologues *arias*, as in an opera. The reason I use the musical term *aria* is there is a musical aspect to dialogue. I like to speak in terms of the characters singing their songs. Each has a certain cadence and rhythm. In particular, we are dealing with the rhythm of each character's speech. Distinguishable rhythms. Again, education, sociological circumstances, background, where the person came from, regionalisms—all have a bearing . . . all these things have a bearing on the particular way this character sings his or her own song. If you have seen a musical score, you have seen that they are annotated; the composer writes in specifics, loud, soft, very soft, whatever, to tell the interpreter how to sing or play those notes or phrases. There are all kinds of instructions all throughout a musical score as to how it should be performed. The composer has it easier than we do because the composer has specific notations and note values that give a particular sound and rhythm to the music, A musical language: *andante, allegro, forte, pianissimo,* etc. We don't have that. We only have words. Phrases. Those phrases not only carry content, there is a musical component to them as well, and it is a writer's ear that is attuned to this musical quotient. So it is not only content that we as writers are concerned with; we are also concerned with—subliminally because we do a lot of this stuff automatically—sound. Understand that we have to identify the sound with the character and the character's background and all the information that we have discovered about that character so that this particular character will sing in this particular way. That is what writers do. The sound, not only the meaning, but also *how* it is said. How it is said has a bearing on what? Its appeal to an audience. Its acceptance by an audience. Its believability. That ability to write believable dialogue as well as engaging dialogue without being wordy makes some writers better than other writers. That's why James Joyce is delicious, at least to my ears. When I discovered James Joyce in university I was like the kid in *A Chorus Line*, the kid who, when he goes through a class with his sister, says, "I can do that! I can do that!"

Sound! Significant for us as writers.

So this is what I want you to do. Take your character, understanding that you have given the character his or her background. You have said the character functions this way, looks like this, has this sociological circumstance, has that psychological situation . . . all of that. You have given the character certain circumstances in which to exist. You have played God in some small way. Not trying to be pretentious, but you do play God. You are the God of this particular story. The character is your creation. And now out of those circumstances, out of that background, you are going to allow this character to speak.

You will also do a pre-history—not a couple of pages, just a short paragraph, at most—that puts why the character is going to say what they are going to say in some context. To remind you of what a pre-history is: It can be anything in the character's far background, which can be ten years ago, an hour ago, or a week ago. Something that has occurred that will have a bearing on why the character will say what he or she says now. The view reminds him of when he was out with his father as a little boy. Anything. Again, make it up. Don't overthink it. Don't justify it. Don't slip into story! So I don't mean just a response to what someone else might have said a minute ago. I don't mean continuity: Someone asks for directions and the character responds with the directions and that's it. No. Something that occurred earlier that connects now and triggers this character to say what she or he is going to say. Use your imagination and make choices. Hear it play out in your head while you are writing it.

This too is an interesting, important exercise that you can always call on if you get stuck in story and wonder, "What the devil do I do now?" You see, I don't believe in writer's block. There are always things that you can do to push yourself beyond or through so that there is no interruption. No stopping of the work. This is one of the ways that you can push yourself to find out what is going on and where you need to go.

Exercise #2—Character Out Loud—Dialogue

1. Write a short pre-history.
2. Place the character in your chosen location (it can be a new one) at a specific time.
3. Let the character speak in an individual voice.
4. Find emotion in the character's song. Don't strain to be profound!
5. How long? Its natural length.
6. You can use sound but not another character's voice. Your character, the character you sketched out in Exercise 1, can be talking to someone next to her or him, or on the phone, or anything you want, but it is the song of one character.

This is their monologue/aria. Who is this person? Let us hear who he or she is.

THREE

The Visual Component—I

We are storytellers and our medium is visual. As screenwriters, when we write a script, what we are doing is telling a story, the motivations and intentions of the characters, the plot twists, the tone of the story, the genre of the story. Perhaps our intentions in telling the story—we might have a particular political or social statement or philosophical statement we want to make. All of which we hope will give a producer and a director reason to spend a chunk of their time devoted to the story we are telling.

If we are lucky enough to get the project okayed, we're also informing an armada of people who have technical needs very specific to their particular aspects of filmmaking. The Casting Director is one of the first people that will see your script. Casting is a major factor in the success of a film. Not simply because of the monetary assumption that big name actors give the film a better chance at the box office but because casting is an art in itself. Like everything related to the creative team, choices are ultimately subjective. Second to directing, casting is key. We are giving the actors dialogue to speak. Believable dialogue, that they enjoy giving life to, that excites them so as to bring their talents to the project. We are also informing the Costume Designer and the Set Designer. And, unlike a novel or any kind of prose writing, there is a camera involved, so the script must be available to the Director of Photography. We are providing a jumping-off point for a sizeable creative team to spin off from and design amazing costumes and evocative sets and all the other details that go into the making of a film. In addition, the Production Manager will create a Shot List from our script that becomes the blueprint for all the technical wizards and the technicians on the shoot.

To this end, screenwriting is a kind of shorthand. And the primary concern is: What does the camera see? What the camera "sees" is what makes the demands of screenwriting different from any other form of writing. This means that technical terms are part of what and how we write. We don't write in prose like a novelist does with the sole purpose of engaging our reader. Writing for film requires a certain specificity. That is why I like to call a screenplay: A Technical Manual Artfully Written. Making friends with these technical terms is unavoidable. Getting comfortable with them is eventually the "artful" part. Film offers a canvas like no other. From grand expanses to intimate insights.

Film Form—Screenplay Format

Because of the proliferation of screenwriting software and skilled marketing, too many beginning writers mistakenly think that learning how to use the software is all that's needed to become a legitimate screenwriter. That is so far from reality that it is almost laughable. You would never think of driving a car with all its gears and gadgets by just reading a driving manual. No. You would have to learn to drive first. I want you to become familiar with the basic terms of Film Form and their application without using the crutch of software. At this learning stage, stay away from screenwriting software of any kind. Software will lead you wrong because you are not familiar with what the terms actually call for. It's critical that you first understand the *logic* behind the language of Film Form.

Below is a full explanation of technical terms used in Film Form and how to use them. I want you to type your Film Form exercises—yes, the old fashioned way—even though it may be a little tedious at first. Getting the layout of the page involves setting a few margins in whatever word processing system you use, Word or Pages or whatever else is out there. Software programs are helpful down the line and necessary when you submit a script. For the purpose of learning the craft, avoid software until the very last couple of chapters, if you must at all. Granted, using the software is easier, faster, more convenient; all those very advantages, however, will steer you wrong at this stage. You will be using shortcuts before you know where you are going.

Screenplay Format

MARGINS	Left 2"
	Right 1"
	Top 1"
	Bottom ½" to 1½", depending on where the paragraph ends.
FONT	Courier, 12 point
	All lines are single-spaced except for a double-space above and below dialogue.
DIALOGUE	Names of all characters are capitalized and centered at the top of a column 3" wide: The left margin is 3¼" and the right margin ends at 6¼".
CAPITALIZATION	Character names at the top of each Dialogue column. And names of characters when they first appear within a descriptive paragraph.

Camera Terms

SHOTS	LONG SHOT (takes in all the surroundings or beyond)
	MEDIUM SHOT (knee and above)
	CLOSE UP (shoulder and above)
	These are the basic and most-used shots and all you really need.
POV	View of what a person *not* in the shot sees.
SLUG LINE	A thread of the designated LOCATION and TIME FRAME.
LOCATIONS	INT.
	EXT.
TIME	DAY (and variations; e.g., Dawn, Sunset, etc.)
	NIGHT (and variations; e.g., Twilight, Midnight)
VO	A voice heard but not seen speaking on screen.
OC	A sound or voice that is part of the scene but occurs outside of what is in the scene.
	Note: Both VO and OC are placed to the right of the character's name in the dialogue column.
CUT TO:	The joining of two pieces of film (shots) end to end. One cuts from one shot to another shot.
	NOTE: The camera can also 'move with' so as to stay in the same shot but gain a wider view or a closer view (e.g., we move in close to see . . .)
DISSOLVE	When the image crumbles.
FADE IN/OUT	Used only at the beginning and end of the film.

There are other terms, but the above are ample enough to write a good screenplay.

Film Form is the visual articulation of the writer's imagination, come alive on the page. The concept of telling your stories based on what you see and beginning to incorporate that into the whole process of telling your stories doesn't come naturally. You have to remind yourself, "Oh, yeah, there is a visual component involved; there is a visual presence involved. I am responsible for the visual content." So, you see, it is not just about writing good dialogue.

I call it The Two Strings concept. You hold two strings at all times: the Dialogue and the Visual. You hold two strings, one in each hand; in one hand, you have the string that controls the visual flow, and in the other you have the string that controls the flow of dialogue. They are both connected by your foot that—just kidding. You also control and write in the Dynamic, which are the few lines of description that run through the script, interspersed with the dialogue.

This is a big step in your transformation from writing in compositional form to becoming screenwriters, and it takes some getting used to. You have to begin to see this stuff. As well as hear it. The exercise for this chapter will be your first stab at writing in Film Form.

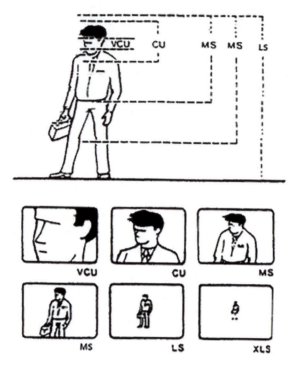

For our purposes, all you will need are three shots: Long Shot, Medium Shot, and Close Up. This diagram also shows other, rarely used, shots.

Now, every scene or SHOT is set up structurally in the same way, using a SLUG LINE.

1. INT. or EXT.: Interior is an enclosed space (walls and a roof) and exterior is outside.
2. LOCATION: e.g., Railway Station Platform.
3. TIME: e.g.—Early evening.

NOTE: The SLUG LINE is always in that order, and on the page it looks like this:

        EXT.—Railway Station Platform—Early Evening

When you change the location, you have to immediately establish where you are again. Tricky, so be aware.

        INT.—Railway Station Waiting Room—Early Evening

Film Form provides a visual road map for the story. It also provides a control mechanism in terms of time frame, so the writer can never get lost, time-wise, in his or her story. In addition, the specificity of time allows the Production Manager to schedule his or her shoot. Film is rarely shot in continuity, making Film Form even more essential to the whole business of filmmaking. Generally speaking, and there are exceptions to everything, most of the Exterior night shots are shot together at night and the Exterior day shots together during the day. Most Interior shots can be filmed at any time. So you see, being specific is also tied to the budget of the film. The closer you are to showing you understand this and the more you incorporate it into how you tell your story the better. Setting up shots also involves time. If you call for ten locations in a ten-minute film, you're calling for too many because your shoot will take twice as long, so your budget will run twice as high. In a ten-minute film, you should limit yourself to three or four locations, at most.

"CUT TO" is an editor's term used judiciously by you, the writer, only when the story calls for a specific moment when, in order to fulfill your intention, you're saying, "Cut the film here. Stop the film here . . . and pick it up here."

SHOTs go on the left side of the page and CUTs go on the right side of the page. The eye travels from left to right, so on the right hand side just below the lines of description or column of dialogue, the last line your eyes have traveled to, is where the CUT goes. And then, as logic would suggest, you must answer the question, "Cut to where?" CUT TO: the left side of the page. Because as you continue reading, your eyes move to the left, so that is where the next SHOT is described: on the left side of the page.

EXT.—Railway Platform—Early Evening

Then you might have some description and some dialogue, and then:

                                          CUT TO:

INT.—Railway Station Waiting Room—Early evening

Cuts are always necessary when you are changing the Location—for instance, going from the Railway Station to a Living Room. You can, however, go from the Living Room to the Kitchen by simply following or moving with a character or making use of OC—the term for Off Camera, a voice or sound from the character in the kitchen.

POV is another term beginning writers get hung up on and often use incorrectly. There is no such thing as a point-of-view Shot. It has got to be *somebody's* point of view. John's point of view, Mary's point of view. The man hiding in the bushes' point of view. The woman behind the curtains, up in the window, who we don't see's point of view. It's got to be somebody's point of view.

POV—From her balcony Mary watches Claudio as he walks across the piazza waving to the shopkeepers sitting outside their shops.

                              MARY—OC
            I see him at the same time every day.

The camera terms indicate that Mary is not in the shot. The camera becomes Mary's eyes, so she's not in the shot. Claudio is in the shot. Now, if you want to include her in the next shot, you would need to add CUT TO: and describe the Shot where we would see her. CUT TO: Medium Shot (let's say) Mary and Mark standing on the balcony, talking to Irv. There is a basic logic to it.

I personally never use camera terms like PAN. I just call for moving the camera. We move with Mary as she walks across the square. I go for a smoother read and leave a lot of camera terms to be inserted or expanded upon by the Director or Production Manager. I never refer to the camera. I try to minimize my technical references. As the writer, I try to keep it to storytelling as much as I can.

Then there is the INSERT. Let's say I want the audience to see the *New York Times* in a certain place in the scene. I would use the term INSERT:

INSERT—The *New York Times* folded neatly on the kitchen counter.

FADE IN and FADE OUT: In the early days, they would fade in on a moment, usually a comic's routine, shoot the routine, then they would fade out; they would fade back in on the next routine. The FADE suggestion is now antiquated. You can use FADE IN at the beginning of a script and FADE OUT at the end of the script.

Dialogue in Film Form—Second Character

We covered the subject of Dialogue earlier in relation to a monologue/aria. Now we broaden out to add a second character. With a second character, what we have our characters say to each other in helping us tell our screen stories requires a closer look. The characters don't say what they might say, what they should say, all that we'd like them to say . . . but only what they must say for the audience to understand what we want them to understand in the way we want them to understand it at that point in the story. As far as the form, there are four elements to consider when writing Dialogue in Film Form.

The character's name—always in capital letters.
The words spoken—always in the center column.
The character direction—always in parenthesis.
The description—always at the left margin.

If you hark back to what we covered in Chapter Two, I said real dialogue is generally boring. In ordinary conversation people say far more than they need to to communicate what they are really saying. It's not only believable that we are looking for, it's the essence of what the characters are actually communicating. Like anything, it takes practice.

Here's an example from the script *The Elephant Is Well* again. The character STU fills out an application for the Magazine Photo Contest to which he's decided to submit his Noble Little Italy portrait. He discovers that he needs a release from the subject to be attached to the photo application. He doesn't know who the subject is. The closing day for the contest entry is rapidly approaching. He goes to the magazine office to plead his case. The Editor in charge of the contest is out for a late lunch. He charms the young assistant.

Script Example

```
INT: UPSCALE JAPANESE RESTAURANT - DAY

MED Shot of man's shoes held in one hand.

                    WOMAN (V.O.)
                (authoritative yet soft)
          You must be disqualified.

                                              CUT TO:

Close-up - STU's Face. Disappointment personified.

                    WOMAN (V.O)
          I'm sorry, Dr. Fisher . . .

Pull out to see STU looking miserably awkward, holding his
shoes in his hand, bending towards a very attractive, severe,
no nonsense young woman, smartly dressed, very sure of herself,
sitting on a cushion in a private cubicle of the restaurant.

                    WOMAN (Continued)
          . . . that you've wasted your time. Rules are rules.

                    STU
                (a last gasp)
          Ms. Kowsky . . . I know rules. I respect rules. But
          sometimes things just aren't so simple.

                    MS KOWSKY
          We take this contest very seriously. No
          contact with aspirants—Thus . . . no tampering.
          I eat alone.

                    STU
                (gasping for air)
          Can't we stretch the rules a little?

He takes a picture of VITTORIA out. She turns her face away.
```

                              STU
                    I promised . . .

She keeps her face averted. He shrugs, turns to leave.

                              MS KOWSKY
                              (softens)
                    A child?

                              STU
                              (a straw)

          . . . A. . .beautiful child. Full of hope and love
          . . . doesn't walk right . . .

MS KOWSKY sneaks a peek at the photo.

                              STU (Continued)
                    . . . it would mean a lot to her.

VITTORIO'S Face.

                              MS KOWSKY
                              (interested)
                    Oh . . . that face . . .

                                                  CUT TO:
STU hopeful. MS KOWSKY studying the face on the table.

                              MS KOWSKY
                    That definitely is a face . . . but I don't see how
                    I can . . .

                              STU
                              (when angels fear to tread)
                    I've taken photos all my life . . . this
                    contest . . . I've never . . . entered before. I've
                    never even tried.

                              MS KOWSKY
                              (strikes a chord)
                    Put yourself on the line . . . (he nods) It's hard
                    to be judged. Nobody likes rejection.

                              STU
                    So you see why I can't be shut out even
                    before I start.

                              MS KOWSKY
                              (admiring VITTORIO)
                    It's all there in his face . . . his whole life.
                    Proud . . . almost noble. He must be somebody.

                              STU
                              (fumbling)
                    Well . . . he's . . .

                              MS KOWSKY
                    No . . . Don't tell me. I don't know. Then you
                    would really be disqualified.

She laughs. He laughs. She casually puts her hand to a hairpin
and shakes out her hair.

                    MS KOWSKY
I've seen a ton of photographs and every once
in awhile . . .
                    (looking at him with measured interest)
You took this picture . . .
                    (STU nods, she studies it)
Sure . . . yet tender . . . strong . . . but
delicate. You know intimacy. I'd like to see how
you handle women.

STU nervously smiles.

                    MS KOWSKY (continued)
          Let me have it.

                    STU
               (surprised)
The picture?

                    MS KOWSKY
The release.
               (STU's face goes blank)
You don't have it. The point is that the subject's
signed release has to be submitted with the photo.

                    STU
This is embarrassing.

                    MS KOWSKY
Try me.

                    STU
He's . . . not easy to . . . approach.

                    MS KOWSKY
               (understanding)
He doesn't know you took the picture and you're
afraid he won't give you the release.

                    STU
               (determined)
I'll get it. Definitely . . . soon . . . immediately!

She just stares at him . . . deciding.

                    STU (continued)
    . . . and . . . and . . . I'm really a dentist.

                    MS KOWSKY
               (smiles like a Cheshire cat)
Candise Kowsky . . . but I'm really a LOLA.

In this scene it is the words, the dialogue, that carries the weight and
gives the scene its meaning.

To go back to CUTs for a moment. In all my years of teaching, there
are always a few who grab on to the idea of CUTs and go a little crazy
with them, cutting every time someone speaks. At this early stage, I want

you to call the CUTs only because it is vital that you begin to sense the *movement* of your story. Later you will call CUTs judiciously, only when they are needed to be accurate about that particular progression because of its intrinsic importance within the story. CUTS control the rhythm of the work. A very fast-paced scene might need a lot of cuts, creating a staccato rhythm. Or, in contrast, an intense psychological scene might need a very wide shot where you move in closer and closer incrementally so you don't cut at all but just follow your characters, creating a steady build to the scene. My insistence on you learning CUTs and using them is in order for you to make the switch from compositional writing to screenwriting.

Writing in Film Form is the big departure from compositional writing. When you start to use Film Form instinctively, you are morphing from a prose writer into a screenwriter. It does take time to get used to. As screenwriters, you have to write from the point of view of what the camera sees. That is what visual writing is. Until you have found your feet as screenwriters, writing in the CUTs and SHOTs will serve to cement that transition. After you become familiar and are writing scripts on your own, you will call CUTs and SHOTs only when absolutely necessary. I also advise you to not go by scripts you might find on the Internet or published in collections. Those scripts have been most likely filtered through many alterations and could be the director's version or the shooting script or who knows what. You might never find a writer's original script—that is, a writer who can be taken seriously.

Screenwriting—The Recipe

What we really want to know is what goes into the stew. The DNA. The tools at your disposal are Description, ample but accurate; Dialogue (the words and sounds we need); and suggestions of specific Shots and the Cuts that precede them, creating rhythm as well as meaning for the screenplay. These things allow you all you need without adding explanation and putting up signposts as to what you mean. You are not writing a novel for the screen, nor a mutated stage play with the visuals plopped in later. You are writing a story specifically for the screen, using the camera to its utmost advantage to help you do that.

Playwriting: The diagramming of physical and mental energy in a prescribed space.

Screenwriting: Related incidents told in a unifying manner from the point of view of what we see; a form of storytelling where the visual component takes precedent over what is said. The old adage goes, "If you see it, you don't have to say it."

Screenwriters have to learn to see and then be able to write what they see, and hear, in the required form for the screen. You approach it as if the film had already been written and shot and is now being shown on a screen in front of you. The screen is inside your head. All you have to do is write it on the page. Easier said than done—and takes practice.

Rule of Thumb: The big shift for you is to remember that the reader of the screenplay can know no more than the individual sitting in the audience watching the film. In a screenplay . . . there is no explanation.

Student Exercise Examples

Here is an example by Jessica, a student in one of my New York intensives. I include it because she has taken a good stab, but there are also mistakes.

```
EXERCISE 3: Film Form - Jessica

INT: BOOKSTORE-DAY

MLS

Polly is sitting at a table drinking coffee and reading a book. It
is a small bookstore. About 5 small round tables are in the corner
with windows looking out onto the streets of the West Village. Very
narrow rows of bookshelves crowd the store. It has a very old,
antique look. A young man, Braxton, is sitting at the table beside
Polly. She doesn't notice him but he keeps occasionally looking
at her, half smiling nervously. He is very handsome. He is Puerto
Rican with green eyes and a lean, muscular physique, 27 years old.
He coughs a bit and squirms in his chair. Polly looks over at him,
he quickly looks down. Polly smiles and continues reading her
book. Braxton moves to the seat closer to Polly, she looks at him.
Braxton takes a deep breath and opens his mouth to speak.

                         Polly
                  (interrupting Braxton)
                         Wait

Braxton looks confused.

                         Polly
                  You are very attractive.
Polly looks at the book Braxton is reading.

                         Polly
                       (smiling)
                  Interesting choice

Braxton smiles and begins to speak. Polly leans over and touches
his thigh before he can speak.

                         Polly
            Would you like to go grab a drink?

                        Braxton
                  (clearing his throat)
                  Yea, uh . . . Yea definitely
Braxton nervously runs his hands over his head.
```

```
                                                            CUT TO:
CL
Polly's face as she smiles facetiously .


                            Polly
                Are you suuure you want to go?

                                                            CUT TO:
MS

A good looking man in a suit around 40 years old walks by. Polly
looks him up and down with a very pleased expression. Braxton is
watching Polly as she does this.


                            Braxton
                          (anxiously)
Yes . . . yea lets go. I know a cool spot not too far from here .

                                                            CUT TO:
CL

Polly smirks.


                            Polly
                (throwing her scarf around her neck)
                    Well ok then, vamanos!
```

Jessica wrote a nice telling moment. Good. Her mistakes are referred to below. She didn't use caps for her character's names. And the directions for the actor should be in parenthesis and before the line.

```
                        POLLY
                (interrupting Braxton before he can speak)
            Wait.
Braxton looks confused.

                You are very attractive.
                    (looking down at the book Braxton is reading)
                Interesting choice.
Braxton smiles and begins to speak again.

                    (Polly interrupting leans over and touches
                    his thigh)
            Would you like to go grab a drink?
```

One more. Johanne. Excellent student. Did a really fine job, but for everyone the Form takes getting used to. This time it's to do with the slug line. When you are in the same location, you don't have to repeat the slug line. In this case, EXT – Cemetery. She is in the same location, so all she needs is the Shot.

Screenwriting workshop   Exercise 3: Film Form –
fall 2014   Visual Component 1
Johanne   Second character

PREHISTORY FOR SECOND CHARACTER:
An American man named Tom, age 46. He lost his 6 year old son
8 years ago. The kid lays at rest at the site next to Archie's
late wife. Today the two men meet for the first time on the
12th anniversary of Iris' death.

> EXT: CEMETARY – DAY
>
> Establishing shot of cemetary.
>
> > > > > > CUT TO:
>
> EXT: CEMETARY – DAY
>
> LONG SHOT of Archie standing in front of a grave
> with a bouquet of flowers in his hands. Followed by a
> MEDIUM
> SHOT of Archie wiping leaves off a tombstone revealing the
> inscription "Ellen Iris O'Hara 10.17.1937 - 05.06.2002".
> Archie places the bouquet of flowers below the inscription
> and gets up slowly.
>
> > > > > > CUT TO:
>
> EXT: CEMETARY – DAY
>
> MEDIUM CLOSE UP of Archie in profile looking at the grave
> vacantly. We hear the sound of footsteps before a man
> enters the frame from behind.
>
> > > > > > CUT TO:
>
> EXT: CEMETARY – DAY
>
> MEDIUM CLOSE UP of the two men standing side by side.
>
> > > > TOM
> > (In a compassionate tone without looking at Archie)
> > > Never get's easy does it . . .
>
> (Archie keeps a straight face)
>
> > > > TOM
> > > That one day a year you wish
> > > you could just rip out of the
> > > calendar . . .
>
> > > (Sighs)
>
> > > > > > CUT TO:
>
> EXT: CEMETARY – DAY
>
> CLOSE UP of Archie
>
> > (Archie is still unresponsive)

                              TOM (VO)
                         Cancer?

                              ARCHIE
                         Ovarian.
                                                      CUT TO:
CLOSE UP of Tom

                              TOM
                    (Nods, comprehending)

                              Happened to my aunt too . . . stage 3
                              when they found out . . . didn't stand
                              a chance . . .

                    (Sighs then turns towards Archie and extends his hand)

                              I'm Tom by the way.
                                                      CUT TO:
EXT: CEMETARY – DAY

MEDIUM CLOSE UP of Archie and Tom

                    (Archie turns towards Tom, shakes his hand and sends
                    him a polite smile. The two men return to their
                    previous positions but Archie focuses his gaze on the
                    tombstone in front of Tom)

                              ARCHIE
                    (Solemnly)

                         My condolences.

                              TOM
                    (Makes a little nod in return)

                              Came home from soccer practice . . .
                              happy . . . a little more tired than
                              usual. . .fell a sleep in front of the
                              TV . . . The next day he didn't wake up
                              . . . a congenital heart defect . . .
                              died peacefully they say . . . (Sniffs
                              and clenches his fists). . .

                    (Takes a deep breath)

                              You have kids?

                              ARCHIE
                    (Apologetic)

                         A son.

                              TOM

                         Grandchildren too I assume. . .

                              ARCHIE

                         Twin girls . . . 8 years next month.

                              TOM

                    (With a crooked smile)

> Ahh double trouble . . . You're a lucky man.

(Tom's smile turns into an awkward look considering Archie's female appearance. Archie sends him and understanding look. Tom kneels and takes out a knitted rabbit from his inner pocket and places it on the tombstone)

> TOM
> My wife makes these. . .

(Ironically)

> They're supposed to bring good luck she says . . .

(Tom shrugs and gets up)

A wind picks up and makes the cherry trees sway from side to side.

> TOM

(Looks towards the sky)

> Looks like it's gonna rain after all.

(Tom zips the collar on his sweater and looks at Archie)

> Was nice meeting you.

> ARCHIE

> Likewise.

Tom starts walking down the gravel walkway. Archie bends down and picks up a flower from the bouquet and places it next to the knitted rabbit.

Now for the exercise. An introductory idea of progression and emotional content, a little stretch. You can work out a simple progression. Keep it simple. Again, this is about learning how to use these new elements of the craft. It is not about winning an Oscar.

Exercise #3—Second Character—Film Form

You have your main character. Now add a second character. Put both characters into a location—one of your locations or a new location. These two characters are going to interact and something has to happen. It just can't be "uh, what time is it Joe? . . . It's three o'clock. . . ." finished. Something has to happen between them, and if it is an expression with an underpinning of emotion: good. This is not like the aria exercise, so you don't have to strain for it. Using Film Form is what this exercise is about.

You have to call the CUTs and set up the SHOTs. You have to move the camera. And I am going to limit you to the three shots: a long shot, which means far away; a medium shot, which means in the middle; and a close up, which means tight, close. You ought to be able to tell your stories with those three shots. You shouldn't have to get more complicated than that.

1. Create a short character sketch for a second character. For example: Stephanie is a small, middle-aged woman, shabbily dressed, who lives alone.
2. Write a few lines of pre-history for your second character. For example: Carlotta has been catching the same train every morning as Stephen (your primary character). She always seemed to be wrapped up in her own thoughts, never appearing to notice Stephen.
3. Find your two characters in one of your existing two locations (or, if you want, a new location).
4. Let your characters interact so that something happens. It is not just an exchange about the time of day. If you can find a simple emotional core for the moment, all the better.
5. Designate a time.
6. Set the scene with a SLUG LINE identifying Interior or Exterior, Location, and Time.
7. Put all your Dialogue in a column in the middle of the page.
8. Call the CUT when moving the camera.
9. Designate the new SHOT that you are cutting to:

Long shot: of . . .
Medium shot: of . . .
Close up: of . . .

Don't move the camera more than you have to. Stay simple. You are not writing the best movie ever made! Film Form is about telling your story in an active form.

Have fun!

FOUR

The Visual Component—II

As writers, you are shifting gears from compositional writing to screen-writing throughout these two chapters on The Visual Component. As one of my students remarked, "It's like turning the sock inside out." The shift takes getting used to, and you will begin to think differently. Film is primarily a visual medium, a blend of the visual and the spoken word. Which one takes precedent over the other is a subjective, artistic preference most often dictated by the director's bent. Some films are very wordy, some rely almost exclusively on the visual. The indisputable reality, however, is that in the case of most, the core of the film is rooted in the story, which is the responsibility of the screenwriter. There are variables to every situation. Sometimes the director will also be the writer or write the script with the screenwriter. The best of all situations is that you are both at least on the same page. In the worst situation, the original writer gets replaced by another writer, and then that writer ends up being replaced by three altogether new writers. I speak of Hollywood, in particular, a world like no other. The position of the writer is a tenuous one, so out of the gate you must understand and be comfortable with Film Form in order to even submit a script and hope for a read.

Because of the importance and complexity of Visual Writing, I have separated the subject into three sections. In the previous section we went into the mechanics of Film Form. In this section, the challenge will be to apply what you learned in a scene that is all visual, without any dialogue.

A Scene without Dialogue

There is no such thing as a writer setting out to write a scene without dialogue. We are not in the era of Silent Film. However, in films with all kinds of sound and fury and good dialogue, there are sometimes moments that are exclusively visual. These moments rely on the visual perception, the visual logic and power of what we see alone, for insights, for emotional content. And, in the case of so many films

49

today that rest heavily on the complexities of technical heft, simply for dynamic impact, this does not preclude sound. In fact, the sounds become emphasized and are more intrinsic to the screenplay. Sound becomes even more important. A car chase is one of the most obvious examples of a scene without dialogue. You have the excitement of screeching brakes, of sirens, of hairpin turns and crashes. You can also see facial expressions in close ups. Anxious, amused, cool. All that is a director's territory. If your script contains a car chase, you need only call for it in broad terms.

In this course, however, we are not interested in the obvious, the derivative, the formulaic. We are looking within ourselves for the contribution our particular originality and talent brings to our work. To make my point, here is an extraordinarily complex scene that worked wonders on film. It is from a script written by a writer I have admired from when I first started writing for the screen: James Agee.

It is important for you to note that several examples I have chosen for this book aren't from the final fully formatted versions of the scripts. This example, which was written many years ago, is from Agee's script of the classic film, *The African Queen*, which was directed by one of the best, John Huston. John Huston and Agee were good friends, and, although Agee was not a screenwriter in the real sense of the word, Huston had tremendous respect for his talent. The script is available on the Internet, I am sure. After the first few lines of dialogue a brilliant use of film and character without a single spoken word.

Script Example—1

```
                    ROSE
       You take sugar, Mr. Allnut, I seem to remember.

                    ALLNUT
          That's right, Miss. Couple o'spoonfuls.
She doles them into his cup.

                    ROSE
          And cream.

                    ALLNUT
          Right.
Rose passes him his tea.

                    ROSE
       Bread and butter?

                    ALLNUT
               (taking some)
       'oh obliged.
He picks up his cup an inch to drink and puts it down again.
Nobody else is served yet. Rose fixes Brother's tea and plants it
beside him. She puts a slice of bread and butter on his plate.
```

                              BROTHER
                             (reading)
                'k you?

Rose finishes fixing her own tea, and helps herself to bread-and-
butter. She lifts her cup, not quite crooking her pinkie, and
sips. Allnut still doesn't move; he is waiting for Brother.
Brother finishes and turns his page, and, without shifting his
eyes, finds his tea with a blind hand and blindly drinks it and
sets down the cup again. Allnut, licensed, takes a big bite of
bread-and-butter and picks up his cup and washes it down. By
Rose's covered reaction, it is clear that she has been taught
never, never to do this, but that she expects no better of such
as Allnut. Allnut sighs wetly and contentedly. This, too, is bad
manners to Rose, but she takes it in her stride.

They go on soberly eating bread-and-butter and drinking tea. The
only SOUNDS are those of china, sipping, chewing and swallowing.
Nobody looks at anyone else. Brother and Rose are wholly, stiffly
reposeful; they are used to this. Allnut begins to get a little
squirmy, like a child in church. The silence makes him visibly
uneasy, but he tries not to show his uneasiness.

All of a sudden, out of the silence, there is a SOUND like
a mandolin string being plucked. At first the sound is
unidentifiable, though instantly all three glance sharply up,
each at the other two, then away; in the next instant they
recognize what it is and each glances sharply, incredulously,
at the other two -- and then again, quickly away; then Brother
and Rose glance with full recognition at Allnut, at the
instant that he knows the belly-growl is his. At the moment
of recognition, he glances down at his middle with a look of
embarrassed reproach. He glances up quickly and slyly -- hopeful
they've missed it -- to find the eyes of both still fixed on him.
The instant their eyes meet they bounce apart like billiard
balls, and fix on the first neutral object they happen to hit.
Then Allnut looks at them again: neither will look at him.

All three lift their cups at the same moment, for a covering,
disembarrassing drink of tea. Rose and Allnut simultaneously
recognize what they are doing (Brother is pretending to read,
misses it, and goes ahead and drinks his), and both, at the same
moment, lower their cups to saucers with an almost simultaneous
clink. Both look away from each other. Brother clears his throat
rather loudly and turns a page. Rose and Allnut reach for their
cups; Brother beats them to it. When Brother has again put down
his cup, Rose -- the tail of her eye on Allnut -- picks up her
cup and drinks, her eyes carefully empty above the cup. Allnut
has his cup again on the way to his mouth when his insides give
out with a growl so long-drawn and terrible that Rose first
flinches, then makes a noise across it with her spoon, stirring
her tea. Brother tightens up like a fist, his first reflex being
that this loud one is a calculated piece of effrontery. Allnut
just endures it, with a look of suffering stoicism. When it is
over there is a tense silence. Allnut slowly, slyly looks up at
Brother; he is stone. He looks to Rose; she is gazing far off
into space. Allnut is quite embarrassed, and knows they are. He
does his best to relieve his own embarrassment and theirs.

```
                    ALLNUT
          (in a friendly, yet detached tone)
        Just listen to that stomick of mine.
There is a silence.
```

To further illustrate what I mean by a scene without dialogue, I have taken a scene out of my own work and also one from a student who wrote a particularly good scene.

These scenes without dialogue, which you will now begin to recognize in movies, are usually not very long. And there is a constant question about them. The question is: What would you say to make it more effective? What would you say to make it more dramatic, comedic, whatever. If the answer is, "Nothing"—that, in fact, if you added something it would detract from the moment—then you have a scene without dialogue.

A scene from my script *The Elephant Is Well*: The lead character of the story, Vittorio, has been accused of doing something terrible—God knows what—and is now being protected by his four friends. They are in their clubhouse, the storefront with the blackened windows, displaying a sign that reads, "For Members Only." All five are sitting around a table. Matteo is the big loudmouth of the group who knows everything about everything. He is the authority on anything there ever was in the world. He's decided that since this is a democratic country that they are going to vote for who they feel should be the leader. Of course, he's quite certain he is going to be the leader. He's a natural born leader. So they take five pieces of newspaper and they all write the name of the person they are voting for and they fold the paper and put it into a hat. Guiseppe is reading them; he takes the first one out, and he reads it, and it is Matteo. Of course it is Matteo. He takes out the second one and it's Matteo, of course, right? Takes out the third one, and it is Vittorio. Now . . . magnanimous, of course. He takes out the fourth one . . . and it's Vittorio. And Matteo's smile is now gone.

Script Example—2

```
INT. CLUB HOUSE - AFTERNOON

MATTEO magnanimous. It's nothing. Nods in approval to VITTORIO.
GUISEPPE opens the fourth.

                    GUISEPPE
          Vittorio.

MATTEO'S smile is gone. (opens the fifth) Vittorio.

MATTEO grabs the pieces of paper and confirms the foul verdict.
He throws the papers into the air. The others congratulate
VITTORIO, pound his shoulders, in "buona Saluda."
```

                          VITTORIO
                       (apologetically)
              Bud I think Matteo is da born . . .
MATTEO gets up and walks towards the door.

                           ANGELO
                   Hey. Where you go?

                           MATTEO
                          (angry)
              Maybe I need a shave, what's it to you.

And he walks out and slams the door. The others all look at
each other.

                                              CUT TO:

INT . BARBER SHOP - AFTERNOON

MATTEO seated in the barber's chair. The BARBER covers his face
with lather. The chair is tilted back. Puccini blares on the
radio. The other patrons wait patiently.

GUISEPPE comes in quietly. He wears a dark pin striped suit and
a fedora pulled down over his eyes. His face is grim. He wears
black leather gloves. He walks slowly to the other side of the
shop. The MEN waiting for haircuts, look up, exchange glances
and run out of the shop.

The BARBER looks up, sees FRANCO and ANGELO quietly come in.
They also wear the dark pin-striped suits and the fedoras
pulled down, and the gloves. The BARBER runs to the side near
GUISEPPE and cowers in the corner. GUISEPPE has his gun drawn.
MATTEO stirs, tries to get up to see what is wrong. GUISEPPE
starts to shoot.

ANOTHER ANGLE - THE DOORWAY where ANGELO and FRANCO also have
drawn their pistols and are firing into MATTEO. The bullets
pound into him and blood gushes out in all directions. The body
twitches and is thrown to the floor by the impact of the bullets.
They continue to fire round after round into the body.

                                              CUT TO:

INT. FUNERAL HOME - AFTERNOON

A LARGE ARRANGEMENT OF FLOWERS Pull back we are in the funeral
home. The chapel is crowded with MOURNERS. The women all in
black. we see SANDRINA, the widow, being comforted.

All of a sudden there is much whispering. Attention turns
towards the doorway. A hush. In comes GUISEPPE, ANGELO, and
FRANCO, still dressed in their murderous attire. They stand
aside creating a path. In comes VITTORIO. He stands tall,
immaculate in a dark double-breasted suit, white shirt and
tie, a black fedora on his head, a flower in his button hole.
He takes no notice of anyone but goes directly to SANDRINA.

                          VITTORIO
                     (his hat in his hand)
              I had nothing personal agains him. I respec
              him . . . a man of honor . . . A GREAT MAN.

```
We hear what sounds like a door buzzer off in the distance.
                         (nods his head solemnly)
             . . . a man of honor . . . a man worthy of
             respect . . .

The buzzer insists . . . louder.

                                                    CUT TO:

INT. MATTEO'S APT . - AFTERNOON

MATTEO seated in the arm chair in his living room deep into his
fantasy. "I'll show them." SANDRINA hurries to the door.

                         SANDRINA
             Alrigh . . . alrigh.
```

There you have a scene with no dialogue. The moment in the club before the scene is the lead-in and the moment back in the apartment is the end of the "scene without dialogue." In that circumstance, what would you say? What would you say to illuminate that moment better? What would you say? Nothing. Nothing needs to be said. Now, and intentionally, it also serves as a moment of confusion for the audience because what they realize later is that it is a dream. It is a fantasy. Feeling slighted, Matteo is fantasizing about his own assassination to make himself feel more important. Like a little kid . . . I'm taking my ball and I'm goin' home.

As I said, you don't set out to write a scene without dialogue but, instead, know how to recognize it and to trust the possibility. It is there in your toolbox. It's sometimes an interesting and more effective way to convey an insight into a character or the dynamic of an emotion between two characters.

To give you a rudimentary sense, not in a scene, but simply of the relationship between the visual and dialogue: Picture a moment where someone in an office has just been told in no uncertain terms that their work is not up to par, sloppy. Instead of adding the words: "You're fired," the next visual could be an exterior with that someone walking out of the building, head in the air, chin jutting, in an obvious huff. That's visual storytelling. You don't have to say everything. Nor should you leave it all to the director.

Now lets look at a couple of students' exercises. First we have Sophia's.

Student Exercise Examples

```
EXT. CONVENT COURTYARD - MORNING

LONG SHOT - a large sprawling courtyard with various levels of
tiled terraces and deep corridors behind tall arches on three
sides. There are hundreds of potted flowering plants all around,
pink, mauve, red and white. In the center are several large,
square, white garden umbrellas and garden chairs around round
tables. It is a beautiful sight.
```

We see Valerie with a lot of camera equipment being seated at one of the tables by a pretty young woman with an apron, holding up a coffee pot in one hand.

Walking through the courtyard, bent over almost double, a nun in a black habit, shuffles and sways like a pendulum on her way up the steps to one of the terraces. Sister Ornella has an ugly spoon face and a big nose. She looks ancient.

> SISTER ORNELLA
> (turning her head side to side and smiling)
> Buongiorno, Sorella Ornella.
> Buongiorno, Sorella Ornella.

CUT TO:

EXT. CONVENT - HEAVY WOODEN DOOR HALF OPEN - MORNING

LONG SHOT - we see Valerie drop her white sweater and purse quietly to the ground. She takes out a camera preparing and adjusting its lens. She moves a bit from one side to another to find a good angle.

CUT TO:

Valerie's POV - in a hand held unsteady way. Over we hear a stillness, a few birds chirping. We see a large vegetable garden. We move to see it is divided into rectangles by stakes and vines and rows of small plants, lettuce, beans and tomato plants. We move in closer and see Sister Ornella in her nun's habit, sleeves pushed up, crouched, next to an empty basket. Her hands are in battle with a plant.

CUT TO:

CLOSE UP - Sister Ornella's face is fierce, she grimaces, muttering inaudible words under her breath. She pulls the plant free from the ground tossing it to the side and falls back on her behind, rearranging herself and wiping the sweat from her brow. We pull out a little to see her cover her eyes with one hand and make the sign of the cross with the other. Her eyes now closed, her lips moving as if saying something as she rocks back and forth in a deliberate motion.

CUT TO:

WIDE LONG SHOT - of the sky just above the roofs of the Convent, a couple of small birds swooping towards us and then flying up.

CUT TO:

MEDIUM SHOT - we see Sister Ornella and hear her softly shooing the birds away. She turns back to the task at hand and starts to make small piles of the different vegetables. She takes the peppers one by one and puts them in a row in front of her. She gestures to them, finger to her lips as if, "shushing" them. Then she takes the tomatoes one by one and puts them in a row to the right of her. This time she waves her finger at the vegetables as if admonishing them. She lays a white cloth down on the ground to her left, then she reaches for the eggplants and places them one by one on the cloth. She

picks up the next eggplant. It is quite large and this one she
draws to her and cradles it to her breast.

We pull in close - to see her face soften and smile. We hear
singing very softly (insert popular lullaby from the 1920's)
as she pats the eggplant. Lifting herself with effort, leaning
heavily and clumsily on one hand, she gets up slowly, still
singing to the eggplant. The eggplant is not disturbed.

We pull out - to a wide shot, still unsteady, hand held, the singing
has stopped. We only hear the environmental sounds. We see her
move over to a stone bench and place the large eggplant in a small
basket. She turns back with the basket in her hand and bending over
she picks up two other vegetables and puts them in the basket.

Over we hear a heavy door slam. The sound startles SORELLA and she looks
across the garden. She runs towards us, flailing her free arm at us.

                    VALERIE (VO)
                  (whispered)
          Shit!

BLACK

    That's a scene without dialogue. A good one.

    I am including another student's exercise to illustrate another point.
Juha was a terrific writer. He was a prominent figure on television in his
country and now wanted to move into writing film. He'd also written a
non-fiction book. Busy fellow. He grabbed onto the process like a pro.
Smart fellow. Now maybe because of this background, he found visual-
izing a scene quite easy, but . . . he overdid it. He tracked the entire scene,
moment by moment, calling far too many Cuts. There are three or four
sections where he could have simply described the action. Remember,
explanation has been taken away but description has not. It takes some
getting used to. You've been driving an automatic; now suddenly you've
got all these gears. Juha's idea for the scene was terrific but his understanding of how to write the exercise was flawed. Being a clever fellow,
as we went further and further into the whole process he got better and
better and, in the end, he wrote an excellent first draft. And . . . not in
his own language. Always got me, that. We had a good time.

    Here is his Scene without Dialogue, with all the flaws. Perhaps even at this
early stage of the process, the mistakes will jump out at you. For clarity, I
have put a line through the parts where he goes too far, where he should have
used simple description instead. And to make a finer point: With a sequence
within the scene that goes back and forth between an Interior location and an
Outdoor location, it is better to call for a combined shot. Example:

INT./EXT.—TOBACCONIST'S MEDIUM SHOT—EVENING

    These subtle shifts in how you tell your story are what make writing
a screenplay different from any other narrative writing. It takes practice.
Contrary to the notion held by many, screenwriting is not just about writing good dialogue with a loose story to hold it up.

Juha - Exercise 4 - Visual writing

1. A pre-history for characters:

Earlier that morning at the cafe SERGIO got his 500 euros back,
but he hates SAMI and has decided that he doesn´t need to see
him anymore.

    EXT: STREET IN ROME - EVENING MEDIUM SHOT

    We see SAMI walking on the street. We hear the sound of a
    SMS. SAMI crabs his mobile from his pocket and glances it.
    He stops abruptly.

                                                    CUT TO:

    CLOSE UP TO MOBILE
    We see the display: "It´s settled. FC Pizza will win. Hurry.
    It closes at 8."

                                                    CUT TO:

    CLOSE UP
    To clock on the church tower. It´s 10 to 8.

                                                    CUT TO:

    MEDIUM SHOT
    SAMI starts to run real fast. We admire his running from
    different angles. Then we see him arriving to the out
    door of his tall brownstone apartment house. We see the
    silhouette of the Colosseum on the background.

                                                    CUT TO:

    INT: THE HALLWAY OF THE BUILDING - EVENING
    Sami runs in through the front door to the elevator.

    CLOSE UP
    The display of an elevator pointing up.

                                                    CUT TO:

    MEDIUM SHOT
    SAMI chooses to take the stairs and run like a hell. Angle
    changes according to curves a couple of times.

                                                    CUT TO:

    INT: SAMI'S FLAT - EVENING
    Sami rushes in and sits to open his computer.

                                                    CUT TO:

    ~~CLOSE UP~~
    ~~To the display of the computer which says: You don´t have a~~
    ~~connection.~~

                                                    ~~CUT TO:~~

~~CLOSE UP TO SAMI~~
Sami looks desperate and covers his face with his hands

                                              ~~CUT TO:~~

~~MEDIUM SHOT~~
~~Sami stands up hastily, goes to the door and disappears.~~

                                              ~~CUT TO:~~

CLOSE-UP
The pile of bills on the coffee table on living room. We
move closer to see the words "You haven´t pay your bill.
In order to re-open the connection contact to this
number . . ."

                                              CUT TO:

EXT.- STREET IN ROME - EVENING MEDIUM SHOT
SAMI runs again. Looks up . . .

                                              CUT TO:

CLOSE-UP
The clock says it´s 5 to 8.

                                              CUT TO:

~~MEDIUM SHOT~~
~~WE see SAMI running towards the SERGIO´s~~
~~Tobacconist´s. (Note: we don't know that yet) He arrives to~~
~~the near distance to the front door of the tobacconist shop.~~

                                              ~~CUT TO:~~

INT./EXT.: TOBACCONIST´S SHOP/STREET - EVENING MEDIUM SHOT
SERGIO notices who is coming. He locks the door, turns the
sign hanging on the door. Then pulls down the curtain which
covers the window.

                                              CUT TO:

~~EXT: INFRONT OF THE TOBACCONIST'S - EVENING~~
~~CLOSE UP TO SAMI'S desperate expression.~~

                                              ~~CUT TO:~~

~~INT: THE TOBACCONIST - EVENING MEDIUM SHOT~~
~~We see SERGIO piling the cigarrette boxes with slow motions.~~
~~He looks satisfied.~~

                                              ~~CUT TO:~~

~~EXT: THE OUTDOOR OF THE TOBACCONIST'S - EVENING CLOSE UP TO~~
~~THE DOOR WINDOW~~
~~SAMI´s fists bounce the window with the loud noise.~~

CUT TO:

INT: THE TOBACCONIST - EVENING MEDIUM SHOT
We hear the banging on the door window, but SERGIO finishes
the cigarette pile and moves behind his desk and pours some
coffee himself from the pot.

CUT TO:

EXT: STREET IN ROME – EVENING MEDIUM SHOT
Sami runs around the corner. Jumps over the fence higher
than his waist.

CUT TO:

EXT: SOMEBODY'S BACKYARD IN ROME – EVENING MEDIUM SHOT
We see SAMI running from left to right toward another fence.
THE LAPPHOUND comes form the open back door and tries to
catch him. SAMI jumps over the fence on the right just in
time while the dog reaches his leg, but only partly. He
disappears behind the fence.

CUT TO:

CLOSE UP TO DOGS TEETH
The dog growls with some pant leg in his mouth.

CUT TO:

CUT TO:

EXT: BACKDOOR OF THE TOBAGGONIST IN ROME – EVENING MEDIUM SHOT
SAMI goes through the back door of Tobacconist's.

CUT TO:

INT: AT THE TOBACCONIST'S - EVENING TWO SHOT
SAMI emerges in. SERGIO splashes his coffee. They stare each
other.

CUT TO:

ANOTHER ANGLE
We see the big clock on the wall. It's 1 to 8. Camera moves
so that we see properly that SAMI goes down to his knees. He
takes a bundle of bills from his pocket.

CUT TO:

CLOSE-UP TO SERGIO'S FACE
SERGIO looks him expressionlessly, then nods.

CUT TO:

MEDIUM SHOT
SAMI rises up quickly, takes a betting coupon from the desk,
fill it and give it and his bundle of bills to SERGIO.

CUT TO:

~~ANOTHER ANGLE~~
~~SERGIO takes the money, watches one of them against the~~
~~light above him, then turns to a machine, which verifies~~
~~the genuineness of the bills. He put them through one after~~
~~the other.~~

~~CUT TO:~~

~~CLOSE-UP TO THE CLOCK~~
~~We see the longer hand of the clock ticking the last few~~
~~seconds until it's on top of the hour.~~

~~CUT TO:~~

~~CLOSE-UP TO SAMIS FACE~~
~~SAMI looks like his on the verge of tumbling down.~~

~~CUT TO:~~

~~CLOSE-UP TO SERGIOS FACE~~
~~SERGIO shrugs but there is a hint of smile too.~~

~~CUT TO:~~

~~MEDIUM SHOT~~
~~SAMI collapses on floor putting his hand to his face. We~~
~~hear him crying. SERGIO stirs his coffee.~~

~~CUT TO:~~

CLOSE UP
We see a bundle of bills lays at the other end of the
verifying machine. Beside it there is that betting coupon
of no value.

Exercise #4—A Scene without Dialogue

This is an important jumping off point, so take your time. Understanding and practicing visual writing is key to being a good screenwriter.

1. Create a character sketch (a few lines) for a second character—the same one from the previous scene or another one. Write a pre-history for your second character, keeping in mind and relating to what we already know about your primary character.
2. Find your two characters in one of your existing two locations or another. Designate a time. Again, the scene can't just be about someone crossing a road with a friend. Something must happen. Find an emotional core for the moment.
3. Do the exercise in FILM FORM. Set the scene with the SLUG LINE identifying Interior or Exterior, Location, and Time. Call the CUT when moving the camera. Select the new shot you are calling for. Use Long Shot, Medium Shot, and Close Up. Use the words, not the

abbreviations, so you become habitually concerned with each choice you make.

4. See if you can picture it in your mind's eye; then follow your own directions. Move the camera to heighten a moment and to convey the desired effect, but don't move the camera more than you have to.

5. There can be NO DIALOGUE. I have had writers say to me, "What about a couple of words?" Well, a scene without dialogue means a scene without dialogue.

Be courageous. Be inventive. Have fun!

FIVE

The Transition

Writing is solitary work. There are no streetlights to brighten your way, no signposts to ensure you are traveling in the right direction. It must all emanate from you. It can be a very bumpy ride. You wrestle with this living thing, this story, through its gestation period and through the birth canal. The world of film constantly demands a new and fresh approach to Film. The only thing the aspiring screenwriter has to offer is her or his individuality. The essence of who you are is what is new, fresh, unique in your outlook and sensibility.

The creative part of filmmaking begins with the screenwriter and the screenplay. The end of the creative effort is in the editors' hands. And I say 'hands' with great deference because some of them have not only extraordinary eyes, but their hands become an extension of their brain equal to the best of pianists' or tennis players'. It is then and only then that a film becomes a 'product' ready for distribution, and the possibility of the dollar signs that dance before a producer's eyes, a reality.

If there is one element of screenwriting that brings the writer closest to the mechanics of the craft, it is the Transition. The Transition is a tool that requires a certain level of proficiency to use successfully, but it is an essential part of screenwriting that you need to know about and know how to use. Getting comfortable with it will take a bit of doing, a bit of practice. Screenwriting is no different from learning anything else. Like driving a car: You learned how to steer the car, how to park the car, how to recognize all the various road signs and act accordingly. You can now drive a car because you have learned to combine all those motor skills and respond to multiple signals and signs appropriately all at the same time. After some practice you can be called a driver. Not a very experienced one, but you can . . . drive. With experience, much of driving becomes reflexive, as it will with screenwriting.

When I taught at the New York University Tisch Film & Television School, I walked into my Basic Screenwriting Class one day and the entire group stood up and sang, "Transition . . . Transition . . ." in one mighty voice. In the previous session I had told them that we would be working on Transitions in the next session. Having told them that I really liked the

Transition and was going to teach it that day, they had done a take-off on the song "Tradition"—from the show *Fiddler On The Roof*. We all had a good laugh. Then, I did what the students expected me to do . . . I sang "The Transition."

Transitions are not—esoteric film punctuation—as they have been referred to, better left unwritten and in the hands of the Director or the DP to make the magic. Transitions are in my mind an intrinsic part of writing the screenplay. As the screenwriter, I am neither just the dialogue writer nor am I writing just a shot list with dialogue. I am telling a story. A story told in a visual medium. I am also a playwright. When I am writing a play, I instinctively switch to telling my story within a confined space . . . the stage.

The Transition Defined

So what is a Transition?

The Transition is a tool, a conduit . . . a clutch, allowing you to shift gears, move in any direction, spin to various locations or quixotically turn backwards or forwards into dream and fantasy. The Transition . . . works, Immediately and Without Question.

What does "without question" mean?

It means that the audience doesn't question how you got them there. They are with you. It is as if you took them by the hand and said we are leaving Earth and we are going to Mars and in that very moment you are going to immediately understand how you got there and without question be ready to continue with the story. It's as if you take them by the hand and you say, "Here we go, I am taking you here. I'm taking you into this dream. I am taking you forward in time. I am taking you back in time. I am taking you from the bottom of a pit to the top of a mountain." You know . . . boom boom . . . and the audience will not get lost. They are with you and are ready to follow you on with the story. If you take them someplace and they are disoriented and say, "What the heck am I doing here?" then you are going forward with the story and they are still back there questioning. You have lost them, and they will never catch up. You can't afford that lapse. So . . . you can't afford to give your audience the question of why, how, what's going on? Where am I? What time is it? How did I get there? No room for confusion.

One of the great tools of the craft of screenwriting is the Transition. The Transition happens immediately because of the screenwriter's construct on the page. We put two abstract ends together to not only link story parts but to deepen, refresh, and push the envelope in unpredictable ways.

The Transition breaks the straight lines of narrative story telling. Abstractions dance across the screen insightfully, robust, soft, and easy, connecting the audience in the way the best of poetry can. A simple straightforward example of one kind of Transition would be going from the beating heart of an embryo during an ultrasound to the beating heart of a runner in a track and field event. I could build a story around that. You never know where ideas come from. But I digress.

The Transition is structurally inventive. It intersects pivotal points. Transitions are small epiphanies, puffs of smoke, a magician's slight of hand, linking constantly new wonders of surprise, suspense, and revelation. It takes careful planning to make those special moments seamless and satisfying. The audience is comfortable and ready to move on. The writer has done the thinking for them, imaginatively, effectively, simply without them being aware of it. The Transition is invaluable in allowing flexibility to the screenwriter and instant recognition and comprehension to the audience—a creative tool at the disposal of the writer.

So you see, with screenwriting, as Jules Verne said, "You will travel in a land of marvels."

So as not to confuse you, I need to point out that the term 'Transition,' particularly in software, as well as in many areas of the industry, is also used to cover a wide variety of technical things like Cuts and Fade In and Out, but from the point of view of the writer, the term refers to an artistic choice.

Transitions are at the artistic discretion of the writer. There are no rules to suggest when and where to use the Transition. Nor is anything written on tablets to tell the writer what form they should come in. The Transition is mixed into the screenwriter's impulse and the particular needs of the screenplay. The secret to using Transitions is to be discriminating and not overuse them. For example, you can generally tell if a first-time director started out as cinematographer. She or he will often overuse visual transitions. Beautiful shots of dew drops on a leaf, or whizzing by walls and walls of graffiti, or the like at the cost of the overall film.

So it is the writer's responsibility to be judicious and use transitions only when they move the story along. When they provide a clutch by which to shift gears without interrupting the flow of the material. It is the writer's responsibility to choose when to use transitions and what kind is appropriate for the particular moment in the screenplay. The Transition should not become a gimmick or a fetish. Because they are such fun to use, writers easily fall in love and transition all over the place, to the detriment of the story. The audience will catch on and turn off. Use the Transition sparingly, only when you need it. The Transition, in its audacity and infinite variety, allows the screenwriter to manipulate the screen story progression to ensure the audience remains involved and interested.

A Coat of Many Colors

Transitions come in all shades, sizes, shapes, colors, and combinations.

- The Visual Transition—The positioning of specific visuals in a precise order to technically create the Transition. The visual images, the prescribed shots, are transcribed onto the page with accuracy as seen in the screenwriter's mind's eye.

- The Audio Transition—The Transition travels on sound. Sound takes you from one scene to a new desired scene, location, or dynamic situation.
- The Combination Transition—What we see and what we hear, one primary, one supportive, combine to create the transition and move us in the story.
- The Transition in the Abstract—The idea Transition is a little more complicated but that's the enjoyable part because it percolates in the dark. An idle reference, a suggestion made in passing, the writer's day dreaming, may be the stimulus to move the story. How the Transition is accomplished is the screenwriter's prerogative. It must conform to the conceit of this particular screen story.
- Time Travel—When moving from Real Time (present) to either Flashback or Flashforward or Fantasy, to a new reality, a transition must take you. When your new business is over, you need a Transition to take you back to Real Time so that the audience is not stuck in the prior reality. If they stop to think "Where am I?" again, you lose them. Transitions on both sides of the new reality will assure the audience's continued interest and involvement.

Script Examples

Here is a visual transition—from my *The Elephant Is Well* script.

It is the story of a misunderstanding between Vittorio, a 75-year-old ex-garbage man, and Stuart, a 44-year-old Jewish dentist who almost causes WWIII. The scene is one of disrespect felt by Vittorio. He lives with his nephew's family, where his grandniece is caught in his bedroom using the CD player given to him on his recent retirement. Maria, his nephew's wife, tells him, "If you want privacy, go to a hotel," and slams out of the room.

```
Vittorio sits on the bed in his small bedroom, mourning his lost
life.
                                                      CUT TO:


EXT. - Vittorio's Bedroom - Night

Rain pounding against the window. We see through the rain.
Vittorio, sitting on the side of the small bed, hunched
over . . . forlorn. Over we hear the sound of the rain and a
faint echo of, "arrivederci," coming from the small
recording machine he holds in his lap.

                                                      CUT TO:
```

```
EXT. - LONG ISLAND EXPRESSWAY - Night
Heavy rain against the window of a car, windshield wipers
going furiously. Stu sits behind the wheel. Pass a sign
reading, Amagansett - 10 miles.
Over we hear the faint echo of, "arrivederci."
```

It is a simple visual transition, using the rain as the conduit. We rode the rain from Vittorio's Mulberry Street apartment to Stu driving on the Long Island Expressway.

The transition is most effective when the connecting points; what causes the transition are close together on the page. Sometimes, as in this illustration, we have to strengthen the transition so we add another element. Here we've added the echo of "arrivederci" from the previous scene to help us move forward.

The idea transition (also from my *Elephant* script). When Matteo is rejected as the "leader of the family," he reacts like a little boy. He takes his marbles and walks out in a huff.

```
                                           CUT TO:

INT. - Little Italy Social Club - Afternoon
Matteo gets up and walks towards the door.

                    ANGELO
          Hey. Where you go?

                    MATTEO
              (angry)
          Maybe I need a shave. What's it to you?

And he walks out and slams the door. The others all look at
each other in surprise.

                                           CUT TO:


INT. - Barber Shop - Afternoon
Matteo seated in the barber's chair. The barber covers his
face with lather. The chair is tilted back. Puccini blares
on the radio. The other patrons wait patiently.
```

So, to track this: I went from the social club to the barbershop on the idea of having a shave to the actuality of Matteo getting a shave. It is a transition set up by the idle suggestion of a shave to the shave itself. The fact that it is a fantasy, as you saw in the scene without dialogue example—Matteo's daydream of his demise—is not immediately clear to the audience, and it is planned that way. As the scene develops, there are many hints that something is not right. The outlandish way the conspirators are dressed, the fedoras, the gloves, the guns, the excess in the "murder." I wanted a momentary confusion. As the story unfolds further, the audience will be ready for fantasies.

Here is a simple audio transition, also from the *Elephant* script. In this scene, Stu has gone to the Photo Magazine to plead his case. He is late with his application and he has no signed release form but is desperate to enter the contest. An assistant has just told him that the editor is out at a late lunch.

```
                                             CUT TO:

STU's face. Resignation.

                         STU
            It's important.

                         KIM
            I am sorry.

                         STU
                 (his most charming smile)
            What kind of food does she like?

                         KIM
            Excuse me?

                         STU

            I mean for lunch. If she was eating nearby . . .
                 (Kim raises an eyebrow)
            I couldn't expect you to tell me where she's
            eating . . .
                 (as Kim turns her head away) Just a wee hint.
                 (Kim turns to him)
                                             CUT TO:

Kim's P.O.V. - Close Up of STU'S best boyish face
accompanied by a disarming shrug.
Over we hear ASIAN sounding MUSIC.

                                             CUT TO:


INT: UPSCALE JAPANESE RESTAURANT - DAY

Close Up of a pair of man's shoes held in one hand.
Over we continue to hear the ASIAN sounding MUSIC.

                     WOMAN (V.O.)
                 You must be disqualified.
                                             CUT TO:

STU'S FACE - Disappointment personified.
```

And, finally, here is a Combination transition—visual supported by sound. This time from my *Mengele* script: Early in the screen story, a two-member team has found an old man, believed to be Mengele, and they are bringing him out of the Brazilian jungle to be tried in the World Court. A ragged band of local militia has, in turn, caught them to hold them hostage. They don't care who they are, they just want the ransom.

CUT TO:

EXT. – Deep Into Brazilian Bush – Hot Day
We see the back of a column of soldiers trudging along.
They look about furtively . . . apprehensive . . . seem scared.

CUT TO:

CLOSE UP – of the tall weeds behind the last soldier.
Slowly, a long pipe pokes through the weeds. Hold on the pipe.

Over we hear a "thwap" sound.

CUT TO:

The last soldier, grabbing his neck, pitching over, falling
down. The soldier in front of him turns, sees what has
happened. He panics, drops his rifle and runs forward.

SOLDIER
(screaming)

      I ivaros . . . I ivaros . . . (local Indians)

Pull Out – to see the others in the column break and run.
Some among them fall from darts.

CUT TO:

Reverse Angle – we catch mere glimpses of the Indians, arms
moving forward and spears flying through the air. The soldiers
haven't got a chance against the ambush they're walking into.

CUT TO:

Their Captain brandishing his pistol.

CAPTAIN
(shouting)

      Aie . . . Aie . . .
             (as he shoots at the phantoms that he
             cannot see)

Po, at the first sign of the Captain's distraction, rolls into the
bush behind a tree. The old man starts to run for the bush. Dov
runs after him. The Captain turns, sees them running and shoots
Dov in the back. Dov falls . . . The Captain ducks behind a tree
to escape a spear.

CUT TO:

Po, very professionally sliding his way to safety.

CUT TO:

The dense bush. We hear the bursts of automatic weapons. We
hear cries and curses in Portuguese . . . then nothing, as we
span the dense foliage where nothing but a bed of lush
green is seen. We see a singular tropical bird fly
peacefully, gracefully through the sky . . .

CUT TO:

```
EXT. - Big Blue Sky - Day / London Bridge - Before Dawn

CLOSE UP - of the spectacular colored bird gliding through
the air. We move in close on the blaze of colors, the browns,
reds, greens, of wings and breast. Slowly the colors spin
and then whirl into a blur of colors . . . Dissolve in the
spinning colors then slowly into the colored lights twinkling
along London Bridge.

Over we hear a telephone ringing.
```

Let's track the scene so far: In the progression from Brazil to London, I used the vivid colors of the tropical bird to take me to the colored lights on London Bridge. It was a simple visual transition that transported me immediately and without question. Let's see what happens next.

```
                                               CUT TO:

INT. - London Apartment - Before Dawn
Close on the telephone ringing in a dark room. Pull back
slowly to see out the nearby window, London Bridge aglow, like
an old fashioned Christmas tree.

                                               CUT TO:

Another Angle - as we move in on the room. The forms become
clearer. A bed, a man asleep, disturbed by the ringing
telephone. He gropes for the phone, picks it up, clears his
throat and raises himself.

                                               CUT TO:

Wolfe Kaufman sitting up in bed, the dawn breaking light on him.

                       WOLFE KAUFMAN
                   (refined strong voice)
              Kaufman here.
```

The misdirection transition—the continuation of the scene.

Po has called to tell Kaufman, the control, the man responsible, what has happened. He is told to go to the Safe House and wait for instructions. Wolfe Kaufman is shocked by the death of his friend Dov.

```
                                               CUT TO:

INT. - London Bedroom - Breaking Dawn
Kaufman hangs up. Stands at the window looking out on
London in the changing morning light. He stands erect.
Unflinching, eyes straight ahead.

                       KAUFMAN
                   (softly, almost to himself)
              "Tell me not in mournful number,"
              Life is but an empty dream,
              For the Soul is dead that slumbers,
```

```
                    And things are not what they seem.
                    Life is real. Life is earnest.
                    And the grave is not its goal.
                    Dust throughout - to dust returneth
                    Was not spoken of the soul . . .
                              (he bows his head . . .)
                                                         CUT TO:
```

His face as he lifts it. His eyes blaze wide . . . His jaw is
set, teeth clenched. He hisses, makes it sound like a curse.

```
                         KAUFMAN
                  MENGELE!
                                                         CUT TO:
```

INT. - Surgical White Room - Morning
Close on simple surgical instruments. A scalpel, forceps,
gleaming clear on a white folded towel. A hand slowly reaches
for the scalpel, picks it up gently, professionally. We
move with the hand as it slowly nears the naked baby lying,
"cooing," in white coverings on the table. The hand reaches
for and grips the baby gently but firmly.

```
                                                         CUT TO:
```

The scalpel moving slowly towards the baby.

```
                                                         CUT TO:
```

A tight close up of a beautiful blond young woman,
contorted in anguish. Unable to watch, she turns, gasps,
her eyes snap shut. Black.

In the darkness we hear the baby cry.

```
                        YOUNG WOMAN (V.O)
                         (moans)
                  Oh . . . Oh . . .
```

Let's examine the progression. I used an idea Transition: Mengele's name spoken harshly, followed by the actuality of what he was known for to complete the transition.

A student in a group, when we got to this point and I'd read it out loud, cringed and turned her head away. She could see the moment. That was already an accomplishment. "Mengele experimenting on a baby. You created Mengele for us by the way Kaufman spits out his name, 'Mengele.' Then you show him doing his worst."

Let's read on.

```
                                                         CUT TO:
```

INT. - Jerusalem Apartment - Morning
Quiet. Close up. The young blond woman's contorted face,
eyes tightly shut. Suddenly we hear the celebrating shouts of,
"Mazel Tov." "La Chaim." The woman's eyes burst open wide and
a smile fills her face.

```
We hear a cork being popped.

Pull Out - on the happy scene of a "bris," the ritual
circumcision, taking place in an apartment in old Jerusalem.
The room is full of happy people of all ages. We see a
table set with cakes and refreshments. We hear the happy
congratulatory shouts, cries, salutations and toasts in a
babel of tongues. A telephone rings in the next room. Mayer,
the happy father goes to answer it.
```

At the end of that scene, Wolfe Kaufman relates what has happened and lays out the new strategy. Story wise, all I needed was the telephone call. I chose to give the information in a more interesting, less straightforward way. I wanted to make it more interesting for the audience even if it meant taking them in the wrong direction. I led them down the garden path setting them up to think one thing while something entirely different was going on. I turned them from the possibility of the horrific to a happy celebration. Rather than be upset, they are relieved and ready to stay with me as I continue the story. I used the transition for the purpose of misdirection to the satisfaction of the audience.

When we write our scripts, remember we hold two strings at the same time. Two strings. One string controls the dialogue, the dynamic, all that stuff: the characterization, the dramatization. The other string controls the visual. And what happens with beginning writers is that they get so caught up in the wonderful words that they are writing for their characters to say that they forget about the visual part. They just lose that string. And I keep saying, you've got to hold the other string firmly, until you are used to your visual string. That's what the new game is about: How do you walk and talk at the same time? How do you see them walking and hear them talking. You have to incorporate both of those factors and do them simultaneously. (You might want to take a look at this clip on YouTube: www.youtube.com/watch?v=E5MK1RgE8cs)

To round off this chapter I want to share this with you.

The father of one of my NYU Film School students had been the president of a major film company. We had the progeny of the film world. They were good young people for the most part and didn't wear their parent's cloaks. The father and his trusted friend and VP had recently branched out and formed a film company of their own. At dinner one night, he confided with his family that at the mega company that he had just left, they had everything from legal and financing expertise to a phalanx of high-powered creative types to advise them on all aspects. Now they found they had unlimited time and a pile of fresh new scripts and left on their own, they didn't know how to evaluate the film scripts.

Hearing her father's predicament, the daughter casually offered, "You want to know about the screenplay, call Irv Bauer."

To make a long story short, I had plenty of experience dealing with high-level professionals and had taught several in one-on-one tutorials.

The father called and we started working together. Twice a week, huddled in a corner of this huge empty boardroom at a long wooden table, chatting like we had just come off the golf course. He was a nice man. A smart man.

He did all the exercises. He didn't miss a beat. We finished. He had a short screenplay in full format and some understanding of how to write the screenplay. We shook hands. "A last few words of advice?" he smiled. I shrugged. "A priceless phrase . . . ?" he waited. I looked back at him and said, "Fool around in your head." He stared at me. Then we both began to laugh.

The Transition is perfect to fool around in your head with. It is highly personal. It insists that you use your imagination. There are no rules of the road and, as the Philosophical Sage of our Age, NIKE, raged: "JUST DO IT ."

Exercise #5—The Transition

1. Choose from your already written scenes, the Monologue, the Dialogue scene with your Second Character, or the Scene without Dialogue.
2. Write the scene that comes before or the scene that comes after. Write the Transition that connects the scenes. Remember, the key is to link them, one to the other, with one of the types of transitions. An obvious one: gunfire on a battlefield to fireworks. Find the transition; then find the link.
3. Write it all in full Film Form.
4. Call all the CUTS and set all the SHOTS.

PART II

THE NARRATIVE ARC

Review

We've arrived at a major turning point in the craft of screenwriting. One you've all been waiting for: the script. To get to that, let's recap where we've been.

We started with character, location, and time frame. Who is this person, where do we find him or her, and when? Then we moved on to dialogue. What do people, our characters, sound like? With each step our characters evolved. We progressed on to the language of film, Film Form, and we added a second character. More insights. More food for our imagination. Learning about the scene without dialogue and transitions we expanded our perception of storytelling into a visual, active medium that allows for endless possibilities. We can leap backwards and forwards in time in the flash of a moment and the audience goes right along with us. We can reveal key information without saying a word. We can go into a character's mind and live out their fantasies. We, the writers, have a trunk full of tools, a sack full of fire and fairy dust at our fingertips. (You might take a look at a relevant clip on YouTube: www. youtube.com/watch?v=rJtEWejb4uE)

You have to be familiar with and understand the pieces and their function *independent* of each other before you can put them together. Before you can use them as a whole. We have more pieces to learn about, to wrestle with as we travel on, collecting and piecing the puzzle together.

The question now is . . . what are we writing about? We don't know. Not yet. I asked you in no uncertain terms to not go to story in your heads. I want you to get used to being uncomfortable. Nothing involving process and craft in combination with—most importantly—imagination, is ever comfortable. Feeling uncomfortable is part of being a writer. You must stay open to changes. You will make fewer changes the further you develop your script until, at the end, it will just be nuances here and there that you tweak and play with.

And then you're done.

Choices. We make choices all the time. Even the choice that we're done is a choice we make.

The only thing you can be comfortable with is your craft. If you keep practicing your craft, you will find the work becomes easier because you know what you're doing. Even when you find yourself unsure of where to go next you will always have tools to fall back on that serve to move you forward. I don't believe in writer's block. There is always something you can do to put you back on track.

So let's now move on to the second part of the process.

SIX

The Idea

We now have an embryo in front of us. An embryo with all kinds of ticks and pulses and limbs and germs; germs of what our story might become. However, before we break into Story, I want to give you a background on the whole understanding of the screenwriter's position in the collaborative world of filmmaking. In the United States, in particular, the writer's place is not only an insecure one, but a diminished one.

The Background of Film

We have to start with the theater. Playwrights go back to the ancient Greeks. Great philosophers—Euripides, Sophocles, Aristophanes—all playwrights. A few of those plays are even performed today . . . *The Frogs* comes to mind. The plays still exist and are revered. We can see them staged and we can still read them. In ancient Greece, plays were performed as a cathartic experience. That was the birth of theater in the Western world. In other cultures, myths of the time were enacted in great spectacle-like events. The experience was intended as a religious immersion. We know, though it's contested, that there was a man called Shakespeare: a playwright of such consequence and influence that he is performed in schools all over the world by teenagers who have had barely a glimpse of life.

Playwrights have been accepted and respected throughout the ages. What we may not know, or what may not necessarily be common knowledge, is that playwrights' work was always subject to change. Everybody changed playwrights' work. Actors' managers changed playwrights' work; actors changed words. There was nothing sacrosanct about the playwright's work.

This was the case in most of the world until something called the Berne Convention, as described here from Wikipedia, came to be:

> The Protection of Literary and Artistic Works, usually known as the Berne Convention, is an international

agreement governing copyright, which was first accepted in Berne, Switzerland, in 1886. The larger umbrella organization is WIPO or the World Intellectual Property Organization.

I became aware of this because, while in Paris working on a musical with my composer and partner in the project, Philippe Gerard, an issue came up, and I said, "How do we protect that?" And he said, "You don't have to worry about that. There is the 'Droit Morale.'" Droit Morale means "moral right." And I thought, "What moral right?" I found out that it referred to the moral right of the artist to control his or her own work and was honored in most countries in Europe and elsewhere. The Berne Convention governing copyright law is a dense subject of study in itself. For our purposes of discussion, know that in theater in America, the tradition of changing the playwright's work continued to be rampant. Directors, a new phenomenon in theater, and actors—essentially, almost anyone—could still change the work.

This is the way things remained until the 1920s, when there was a very strong group of American playwrights—Eugene O'Neill, Maxwell and Sherwood Anderson, Sidney Kingsley, and Edna Ferber were a number of them—who changed the status quo. They were the significant and successful playwrights of the day. Broadway was thriving on their plays. These gifted playwrights, these iconoclasts, got together and declared that they were tired of their work being distorted by anybody and everybody and that they were going to withhold their work until they got an agreement from the producers stating that no one else has any right whatsoever to change their plays.

The Dramatists' Guild

That was the beginning of the Dramatists' Guild, which is not a union; it is a guild.

In the early 1920s, what had been the Author's League of America split into two groups: one representing the interests of writers of radio and stage drama and the other for novelists, nonfiction authors, and magazine article writers. The important thing about the Guild is the contract that protects the playwright's work. At the time, the producers accepted the contract because they were under the gun of this extraordinary pool of writers that threatened to shut down Broadway. In that contract, "droit morale" was paraphrased to: "The playwright owns his or her own copyright." The birthright of the work. The contract states that nobody can change the playwright's work except for the playwright or with the playwright's approval—written approval, not verbal. It is not the only contract in use, but no playwright in his or her right mind would consider signing any other contract. A victory for American theater.

Do playwrights always use the Guild contract and do they always stand firm? No. With the proliferation of Off Broadway theaters bursting at the seams, with over 6,000 registered members, and with all the large sums of money and large personalities involved, all too often playwrights, not of the caliber or experience or commanding strength of the original group of pioneers, who are not confident enough to stand up to producers or directors, go along with their work being changed all the time.

In Europe, however, and in most of the Western world, where writers have been held in high esteem for centuries, the Berne Convention is an adhered to and honored agreement.

Film and the Advent of Sound 1927–1930

Unlike theater, film does not have a centuries-old tradition. Film is only a little over 100 years old. In the early days of the Silent Era, film was a novelty. Little houses, for five cents—people would go in and watch a reel. The reel would be accompanied by a pianist or even an orchestra in the pit. It was just a novelty, a throwaway. Nobody wrote film. Occasionally there were captions; it didn't matter who wrote them. Then along came synchronized dialogue in the late 1920s. Now someone had to write something. Actors were going to speak words out loud. This was the big transition in entertainment from the stage to film.

The infant film industry in America reached out to playwrights and novelists because they had some experience with words. There was a voracious appetite for their contributions in the theater and in literature. They were proven, and, yes, Hollywood, right from its early days, liked proven. But we've heard the horror stories about how the novelist F. Scott Fitzgerald, of *The Great Gatsby* fame, and all the rest of them were treated. What we don't know is whether these writers knew anything about film because at that time, nobody knew anything about film.

Film has matured as an art form, and it is an art form. Film producers and distributors were already the key players so that by the time there was a Writer's Guild for the film industry, writers had little power and, as a result, there's no teeth in the contract to protect the writer's work as there is for playwrights. The screenwriter's contract contains a clause that states that in no uncertain terms will the "droit morale" be considered at all. They all phrase it differently, but that is what is meant. The screenwriter does not control the copyright; hence, the writer can't say "boo" once he or she signs that contract. There is a lot of money involved in making a film, and the attitude from the producers remains, "It's our money! Why would I give writers any authority over the work if I am paying for it?" That is why you often see three, or even seven, writers on a film. They can do that. They don't even have to inform the writer. They just fire him and hire her. That's the way it is. A screenwriter's life is a rocky road. Film is a difficult industry to be in. It is not unusual that a good film, a film with integrity, has taken five to seven years, or even longer, to get made.

Now having said that, and suggesting that it is a difficult field, if I didn't think it was still possible, I wouldn't do it myself. I think film can be a wonderful art form if the writer approaches his or her work with a solid sense of craft and work that he or she can stand behind confidently. Given all the other elements, luck not being a small one, the screenplay can be the most compelling aspect of a good film.

This is why you have got to write a wonderful script. Otherwise, you are not even in the ballpark. You have to know how to use the material . . . know how to use the métier. That's the reality.

People want stories because, from earliest times, human beings have had a built-in need to understand who they are and what life is about. Whether it is a light comic story, a serious drama, a suspense thriller—at the end of it, you want to have understood something. It is a way we understand ourselves. Stories, whether in the form of the written word or stage plays or movies, are cathartic. That was the purpose of Greek drama and of the religious epics in other cultures.

"Jake and Sadie lived together for 50 years, small life. They liked each other, so it was a happy life. Didn't have a lot of money, but it didn't matter because, as I say, they liked each other. One day, Sadie gets a cold, and since they didn't believe a lot in doctors and they didn't have money for specialists, they let it go. And she gets pneumonia. Then pleurisy, and unfortunately soon after, she dies. Jake is devastated and, not surprisingly, shortly after he gets sick and succumbs; he dies. And he goes up to heaven.

And there's Sadie waiting for him. Sitting on a cloud. And she says, 'Jake, this is great, this really is heaven, wait until you see.' And he says, 'Yeah, well, okay.' And they go around a cloud and there is the amphitheater in the sky, and she says, 'You know how I always liked to go to concerts but never had enough money, and we couldn't go, and it was hard. And when we did go we sat way upstairs and I could hardly see. . . . Well, whatever I want to hear, whenever I want to hear it, it is always playing. The greatest conductors are here: Toscanini is here, Karajan, Masur came up a little while ago! It's great! It's heaven!' And he mumbles, 'I am very glad for you, Sadie.' And she says, 'Not only for me, Jake, for you too! You know how you loved golf, but the greens were too expensive, we didn't have any clubs, you never played as much as you wanted to, you always felt deprived. . . . I felt bad for you.' And he says, 'Yeah, I did . . . I . . .' And she says, 'Wait a minute. Come with me.' And they go around two more clouds and there's the fairway in the sky and she says, 'You can play with anybody you want. The Scotsman that invented golf is here!' He says, 'Great.' She says, 'And wait 'til you see where we are going to live.' They get into a golf cart, they go around two more clouds, and there's the condominium in the sky. They go inside. Big spacious place, bay windows, as far as you can see . . . blue skies and sunshine . . . it's heaven. And he says 'Yeah . . . very nice.' Wonderful soft furniture. The four-poster bed they'd always wanted. Terrific place. He mumbles, 'Yeah. Nice, very nice.' And she says, 'Wait until you see the kitchen!' Magnificent kitchen. 'Floor to ceiling refrigerator—all the food you ever loved!' And he's goin', 'Whey whey whey . . .' She's saying, 'Bathrooms . . . showers . . . Jacuzzi . . .' And he's going, 'Whey whey whey . . .' And she says, 'What's the matter Jake? This isn't good enough?' And he leans into her. And, in his quiet way, he says, 'If it wasn't for you and your God darned brown rice we would've been here years ago!'"

Jokes are very specific. The right amount of information, told in a specific order, tells your audience what is being made fun of, shares the insight in a succinct way. Some people have a natural instinct for telling jokes. Brevity is called for. Specificity is called for. Rhythm is called for. And when you do that, when you conform, you get it right and your audience appreciates it with you. They know what you are making fun of, what you are indulging in, they laugh with you. We talk about "getting" the joke, right? Your audience gets it. Why? Because you craft it just right. Sometimes the set up is short, the build is long, the pay off is short. Sometimes, the set up is very long, and the build and the payoff are both short. It varies, depending upon the material, where the emphasis is, and what is being related. But you have to conform what is being related into the structure of the joke.

How often does it happen where someone you know tells a joke and it falls flat? Why? Because they pad the set up, or make too much of the build or—the worst—they forget the punch line, the pay off. Much of the art of telling a joke relies on rhythm. As does storytelling.

Narrow Your Focus

So how do we start? We have collected a lot of material. Now how do we get into the storytelling aspect, the narrative part of writing? This is where the romance of being "a writer" fades for some. Why? Because now you are at the first stage of organizing your material, and this part is work. Tedious, perhaps, but essential work.

In my case, when working on my own projects, after my prewriting phase, after I've gathered all the material that has occurred to me over the past several weeks or months (I have found I need three months), I now take everything I have in my little numbered notebooks and copy those notes—those unrelated pieces of information, inspiration, observation, whatever has come to me—into 5 × 8 composition books. Yes, by hand.

In the process of copying the material, it enlarges on me. A couple of lines will end up six lines, eight lines. Eight lines will become half a scene. A half a scene will become a full scene. Just the copying seems to bring it back to me and expand it.

Then what I do is I take all this stuff in the composition books and I type it all out. Yes, again. So now I've gone through the material three times. And, each time, it has enlarged on me. It has also served the purpose of bringing me back to the material: What did I mean two months ago when I made this note?

It is not unusual for me to start a project with a hundred pages of typed, unrelated notes. Notes made with no understanding, no concern as to where the material goes, how the notes work, where they fit, no continuity, nothing. Just a hundred pages of notes, chunks of unorganized material.

I have this mass of stuff and I am going to organize it. How am I going to approach this task?

It may seem a tall order. Order out of chaos. Perhaps not the greatest of sages, but to quote Mark Twain: "Prudence and recklessness go hand in hand in the contract you make with yourself—the rest is chaos." The process gives you a way to manage the task.

In learning the process you haven't got one hundred pages like I usually have, and your prewriting phase consists only of the exercises you did in the first part of this book. In doing the exercises, you applied and practiced each aspect of the craft on the page. In doing so, you generated some material. So, out of that accumulated material, we will now craft a story.

I started you with the discussion of Character because in the real world you will most likely have your own idea, or will have been given one if it is a commission, and, as I emphasized in the first chapter, I always start with character. Why? Because character leads you to story. The subsequent exercises you worked on in the first part of the book would also be part of how you would work if the project were an actual one. However, you won't be considering them in any necessary order. Often the dialogue exercise will be part of what you add to your exploration of character. The third, fourth, and fifth exercises are all necessary tools to be familiar with before proceeding on to narrative. They are all tools at your disposal now.

The Mechanics of Storytelling

For storytelling structure, rather than Act One, Act Two, Act Three, I like to use Set Up, Build, and Pay Off.

1. This is the Set Up; this is what I am setting up. I am introducing the main character/s. I am introducing the central dilemma of the lead character. He or she will eventually have to deal with it in relation to the other characters, and that can be introduced. Or, depending on the story, you may not have him or her involve the other character/s in the dilemma until the Build. The Set Up is who they are, where they are, and how they relate to each other.

2. In the Build, you are saying: I am now going to convey certain information and insights to tell you the situation they are in. The Build

shows the central problem of the lead character and the implications in relation to the other characters.

3.   In the Pay Off, having set the characters and situation in motion and built onto that situation in your chosen order, you now say: I will share my insight with you—the reason why you, the audience, has stayed with me for two hours—so you will understand *this*, the resolution. The Pay Off.

As a storyteller, I am doing something specific within each segment. I am setting up this, I am building this, I am paying it off with this. Those are the simple mechanics of storytelling.

Set Up, Build, Pay Off

You have been working with a panoramic landscape; now you are going to focus in from all that material to find the central idea of what that material suggests. The possibility of an idea. Something that your short film *could* be about. An idea that you can begin to articulate in three separate paragraphs. In its general terms, based on the concept of the Joke, label each paragraph as Set Up, Build, and Pay Off. You might feel hard pressed to see how these pieces will come together as a story, but believe me, with a little attention and imagination, you can make a story out of almost anything.

Now take the exercises that you have already done and use them as pieces of a puzzle. Put them on a table, spread them out, and say to yourself, "What does this suggest to me? What kind of story idea can I conjure from this material?" You don't have to use your complete exercises; you can use parts. You can use fragments of them. This exercise of the Set up, Build, and Pay Off is written in compositional form so you can explain a little and you can do a little background. I say "a little" because with a short film you are writing a paragraph, at most two, for each of the three divisions of the Idea.

Title the exercise: The Idea. Then write—yes, actually write—the words 'Set Up.' Below that, write a paragraph on what you think the set up to the idea is. Below that, write the word 'Build,' and write a paragraph on what you consider the build to your idea is. Likewise, write the words 'Pay Off,' and write a paragraph on the pay off to your idea. What you are saying is, "Generally, parenthetically, at this moment, subject to change, this is what I think my Idea is. I think I am going in this direction." You know it is going to change, but this is the first step in getting it down into some kind of shape.

Wild Card . . .

As you are working, you may find that in order to make sense of the Idea from the limited material you have at your disposal, you need one more scene. A scene that has not been written yet, that we have not heard before—still about the same characters, the same circumstances. It is your

Joker card. So for the purposes of the learning process, you have leeway to write *one* more scene. One more scene—not two, not three. You can just sketch it out loosely; that's fine too.

Now, I've had writers bring in material that has no relationship to anything they have already written. They'll say, "It makes a better story." That's not the point. The point is to use the material that we have generated in the exercises with the leeway to use *one* more scene. Make sense of it. Remember, this is the beginning of your exploration of narrative. I want you to stretch your imagination, stretch your understanding of how to use and implement the *tools* you are now familiar with. At the same time, I want you to focus your understanding of the process and the tools available and to not wander all over the place. This is for you to explore screenwriting as a discipline and its various options: visual, sound, characters, going backwards and forwards in time and/or into fantasy. Work with all the tools film offers. And work with your imagination. Focus it down to an Idea with a Set Up, a Build, and a Pay Off.

With the next and every subsequent chapter we will have plenty of time to go further and deeper into our story until we get to the point where we are ready to write our First Draft. This process, my process, has three junctures where you can check yourself. Writers, for some reason, want to know immediately: "Do you like the material?" There is a process involved, and this is the first stage of the narrative process. It's a hard concept for beginning writers to come to grips with. Trust me, relax into the Idea and you will be doing yourself a big favor.

Questioning

Another concept that beginning writers have difficulty with is questioning their own work. Writing is only one part of your function as writers; the second part is that after you have written what you are working on, you have to step back and question your own work. Do I like it? Do you? You have to ask yourself. Well, you might say, it has possibilities; I don't like the beginning. What do you then? You fix it! Make it better. Question yourself. Question your own premises . . . question your own impulses . . . question your own intelligence . . . question your own imagination . . . question your own idea. Going forward the questioning is going to be the second part of *every* exercise you do. The more you question your work, the more familiar you will become with the mechanics of storytelling. You must cultivate the practice of questioning your *own* work.

Here are several Idea exercises by students to get you thinking. Each one of these was written at exactly the same juncture in the process, and bear in mind that they too, were working from a limited amount of material that came out of the first five exercises.

Student Exercise Examples

Andre F.
Spoleto, Summer 20 I 0

Assignment 6 .

THE IDEA

SET-UP
Sergio's parents are hosting a small dinner party at the
house. Amongst the others they've invited their cousins, Sonia
and Ted, who've brought along their daughter Margo. We hear
faint music and inaudible conversation coming from upstairs.
A small note from Sergio's father *is* slid under his bedroom
door informing him that Margo is here. Sergio frantically and
nervously readies himself to greet Margo.

BUILD
Upon entry into the living room where the party is taking
place, Sergio remembers. We transition to a grainy, clouded
memory he has of having tripped in running to meet Margo
as a young boy. This memory includes us seeing Sergio's
saddened-faced mother do nothing to help her son, and his
father shaking his head in. We transition back to the dinner
party, where Sergio, still fresh with that memory in his
mind, knocksover a vase in his approaching Margo on the
couch. Sergio's father merely shakes his head in disappointed
disgust. Sergio storms out of the house to a park down the
street where he sits upon an elephant shaped bench—one he used
to climb regularly as a child.

PAY-OFF
His mother, concerned, storms from her dinner party and
follows him. On the bench Sergio and his mother sit. She
embraces him and gives him the following directive: Tell me
three things about the man you would like to be 10 years from
now. He lists them: Confident, handsome, and . . . *in* love.
Next, Sergio's mother tells him to "go back in there, and be
that person now." To wh1ch Sergio wipes his brow, and with a
new found confidence, returns to the party. Next, we see Margo
in laughter, donning Sergio with affection and attention.

DONATA- EX 6-IDEA

THE"MESS-AGE"

SETUP
Emma is an old teacher. She comes from a little country-
town in South of Italy but now, to keep on working, she moved
to Rome, just one of those big cities she hates so much and
she think she couldn't live there. So actually she's working
into an high school in Trastevere attended by students coming

mostly from upper class families. Emma is living into the house of old aunt Oelia who was never married and who's invading continuously Emma's privacy.

BUILDUP

The approach with the classroom is a disaster. Students always talk about their beloved teacher Bertelli who unexplainable went away. They seem to hate Emma and, although she does her best to do a good work, they act like enemies. They also stole her cell phone from her bag during a school travel. The worst one is Filippo, the "bad leader" although Emma thinks he has good skills in analyzing and he seems to be sensitive. Last day of school travel, Filippo secretly gives Emma her cell phone back

PAYOFF

In a very restless meeting between students, Filippo, who has read all the text messages in Emma's cellphone and he has changed his mind about her, reveals he told a lie. Emma stole Mrs Bertelli's desk because she's a friend of the head-teacher. It was just a bad joke. Mrs Bertelli simply went away to reach someone important for her life, so it's not Emma's fault. She is probably a good teacher and she needs to work, so maybe she deserves a chance. When Emma enters into the classroom for a new lesson, on the blackboard there's a message for her "Forgive us. Let's start again!"

EXERCISE 6 - SUZI

TITLE: THE BODHI TREE (a Fig tree native to India and South East Asia, regarded as sacred by Buddhists, known as the tree of knowledge)

THE SETUP

Sophie is worried about her younger sister Juliet, a beach bum living in Thailand who constantly asks her for money to fuel her partying lifestyle. Particularly exasperated during one phone call, Sophie resorts to sarcasm resulting in Juliet slamming the phone down on her. She doesn't hear from her again and after two months of silence makes plans to go to Thailand, with her best friend Zoe, to find her missing sister.

BUILD UP

The beach cafe in Thailand, where Juliet was working two months ago, is the first place the two women go to when they get to Thailand. They have dinner together whilst waiting for the cafe owner Scott, an ageing. and gentle American hippy.

He arrives and joins them for a drink re-assuring them in soft, easy tones, that Sophie was 'clean', healthy and happy when he saw her last working in his cafe, two months ago. He tells them he thinks she just went off to another island to get some space and maybe have a break from the partying. Sophie reacts with some degree of astonishment, as her sister appeared anything but healthy, happy and drug-free the last time she talked to her.

PAY OFF.
The two women walk along the beach together and discuss their conviction that Scott is lying or hiding something. They reach a hammock swinging between two Bodhi trees. They recognize it as the one Juliet was photographed in when she first arrived at this beach. The two women sit in the hammock staring out to sea in companionable silence. Suddenly, a lone, small Buddhist monk, resplendent in orange robes, walks into their view. He turns round and both women gasp. The "monk" is a young woman, with piercing blue eyes and a completely bald head. It's Juliet.

Luiz Antonio
July 2012

Screenwriting Workshop – Session 6: THE IDEA

"AN ART FORM"

SET UP
BORIS is a 66 year-old Bulgarian. Intelligent, charming, he works at an art gallery in Chelsea as a Head Curator and became passionate for art. BORIS used to despise the USA and all western civilization, but now that feeling has shifted: he simply hates uncultured people, specially the ones with money. At Times Square he shows us how he feels about these people. He is a former member of the main Bulgarian intelligence agency (an skilled ex-spy), living in New York. He came to the USA disguised as a persecuted Art and Philosophy teacher.

BUILD
Being an art lover, BORIS believes he has found a true art form: to lie perfectly, to create another life.
He supposedly did it in the past, transforming the eastern spy he was into this new art guy. But, since he cannot be a spy anymore, he manages to create another self for him: a clairvoyant, a Tarot fortune-teller.
It becomes easy to find clients among his buyers and he starts to use his old abilities (mostly, the violent ones) to make everybody believe he has "special powers".
JOHNSON, a Wall-Street type of guy and one of his buyers, becomes his first victim, at BORIS gallery.

PAY OFF
At the end, BORIS does not know who he really is anymore. Was he truly a spy in the past? Can he predict the future for sure? Does he know anything about art at all? BORIS pulls one of his Tarot cards from the deck: it is Death. In the gallery, a huge installation is being placed. The art piece falls on him and kills him.

Exercise #6—Idea

1. Take the information generated in the exercises and place them in front of you as if they were pieces of a puzzle:
   - The description of the Characters—the *who* of the story.
   - The Locations that the characters are involved in—the *where* of the story.
   - The Time Frame the story occurs in—the *when* of the story.
   - The Monologue/Aria—the main character out loud.
   - Dialogue, the interaction with the second character—in Film Form.
   - The Scene without Dialogue—focusing on the visual component.
   - The Transition—the scene before or after an existing scene with the *transition* (the clutch) that connects them.
   - Add one additional scene, a "wild card" to help round out your IDEA.
2. Using all of the pieces in whatever way you want, come up with an idea of what your story is. Write a short description in compositional form of what the story is in three parts. The three parts should be headed:
   - Set Up: Using your main character as the foundation, what are you "setting up"?
   - Build: Make a choice and build from your foundation in a specific direction.
   - Pay Off: What is the resolution; how does your story end?

Note: A paragraph or two at most for each.

3. Step back and *question* your Idea. Remember, you are telling a story in its generalities. Does it make sense? Does the progression work? Does it build? Is it interesting? Is the Pay Off clear enough? You will have two more junctures to tighten up and focus your story. This is a first step, but you still need to ask the questions.
4. Based on what you find in the questioning, fix, adjust, rearrange, change it around to improve your Idea. If your questioning makes you rework your Idea, all the better.

Rewrite: Rewrites help you clarify and sharpen your work to *yourself*. At this stage, you are the only one to be concerned with. Remember, if you start showing your work to friends or others, you will only get confused because everyone has an opinion they are all too eager to share. Dangerous.

You are the sole writer. Getting a grip on the process is a way of focusing and strengthening your thinking.

SEVEN

Story—Step Outline

On countless occasions, I've had people tell me they have a terrific story, could they either tell it to me or could they send me what they have written. Unfortunately, nine times out of ten, what they have is the background of a story not an actual story. Something that might have a story embedded somewhere within the generalities of what they think is a story. Another very frequent understanding of what people think is a story is, in fact, an incident. An incident that could perhaps be the germ of a story, but not a story by itself. The background, an incident—those are kernels of possibilities and frequently, yes, they are how a story suggests itself in your imagination and provides a reason to go further and possibly develop them into a story.

However at this point in our learning the process we have gone beyond the random unrelated note taking. Now that you are equipped with the basic tools of screenwriting, you are ready to move on to Story.

What Is Story?

Story is the verb aspect of the telling. It is *what happens*. It is the activity of what happens. It is not the narrative background of what happens. It is not the characters' backgrounds. It is not the explanation of what happens. It is simply the activity of *what happens*, and that is why I say it is the verb aspect of storytelling. As writers, we play detective. Always looking for clues to build our story on. Or you can say we do what the scientist has to do before publishing "the theory of" something. Scientists get an idea. They try combining this chemical with that or various mathematical combinations. They prove out their theory and eventually arrive at the culmination of what began as an idea, and only then do they have something they can publish as a "theory of such and such." We do the same thing. A writer's mind, a creative mind, is always making associations. Always asking, "What if . . . ?" Connecting the dots.

Here is where the fun of being a screenwriter begins. How are we going to mold this clay? All this material we have collected. If you recall, I spoke of a whole cloth from which you cut your pattern. This is where you begin to design your story, to cut your pattern. So our next step after the Idea is to focus our material, the whole cloth, down to the specific activities, the pattern. What happens in the story that we have just committed to in our Idea, in the form of a Set Up, Build, and Pay Off.

Step Outline Defined

Harkening back to the Joke, we use the same format in creating a Step Outline. We look at the Idea and we distill it down to the major activities that we say are important moments in our story.

What are the major turns in the story? Who does what when? Sam tells his brother he is going to China. Sheila realizes she must leave her husband. The big pieces that move the story along. We are working in short form but the process would be the same for a full feature as well. You simply would have accumulated more material, more things happening, therefore more steps.

In the Set Up, from the first paragraph in our Idea, we extract the activities into Step 1, Step 2, Step 3, Step 4. It doesn't have to be four; there may only be three. One line—at most, a line and a half—for each step. Remember, I am not talking about the explanation, the why's and wherefore's. Only the major turning points in the Set Up.

When I write my Step Outlines, I double space between each activity, each step. I don't bunch them up. People think that they are saving space; there is no reason to save space. You need the space on the page to be able to clearly follow the logic of each step and how it leads to the next one. Again, we are working with limited material so you may have three, maybe four, major activities at most in the Set Up. A line or two, not a paragraph. Why? If you have too much information, it tells you that you haven't found the gear that propels your story forward to the next step yet. You need to see a clear thread in its leanest form.

Then you move on to your Build and do the same thing: What are the major happenings in the Build? This happens . . . this happens . . . this happens. Then move on to your Pay Off: What are the major things that happen? You won't have a lot of steps because you haven't got a lot of material. I am not going to spoon feed you as to what 'things that happen' make a good story. Writing is not just an intellectual exercise. You won't get anywhere if writing doesn't ignite a passion, an excitement, in the discovery.

Now, the Step Outline does not include e-v-e-r-y single thing that happens. "Brad tells Steve he is leaving the company." Something happened; it's an important thing. "Steve hangs up the phone" is not. Just the big turning points in the thread of your story. This is where we expand our Idea. This is where we start chiseling into specifics. What are the key turning points in my story? What do I really need?

As you work down your outline, what you may find is that when you articulate the steps, you actually have three steps in the Set Up, four steps in the Build, and only three steps in the Pay Off, when you thought you had four. So you now have a ten-step Step Outline.

Creating the Skeleton

The steps in the Step Outline provide the story Structure. The skeleton. What you're saying is: Out of the idea, written in an overall way and including some explanation, background, and some activities, all written in compositional form, I now have a step-by-step progression to my story. There is no background. There is no detailed explanation. Just the structure. Just the bare bones. Much like building a house. You've poured the foundation, you put up the frame, and you have a roof. Later, you'll add the walls and everything else.

You'll congratulate yourself and say, "I have taken one giant step towards story. A skeleton with no flesh on it. I don't know what that looks like yet, all I know is that I have the bones of the story." Good feeling. From the general approach in the Idea exercise, you've focused, extracted, isolated, identified, the main developments of your story in the form of a progression.

The Step Outline is an exciting stage in the process. Your story is coming alive. You are the God of this little universe. It's here, in particular, where you must be in unison with the heartbeats of your characters. Earlier I spoke of having to hold two strings. Having to see and hear at the same time. Now, as the creator of this story, you must add, "feel." You must feel the progression. You're all in. Take the ride with your characters. You'll step back later.

The Step Outline is a critical part of the process as a screenwriter. You will find you come back to it when you are doing your rewrites. It's what you come back to, to reassess. It is where you make mistakes in logic. It's the tool most professional writers rely on in any medium. In screenwriting, you are revealing your story both verbally and visually, building your story in a different way than if you were writing a novel. Big difference. So in writing for the screen your Step Outline must reflect that.

You will hear a lot about Act One, Act Two, Act Three. That is the most common reference to an outline. As a writer, a storyteller, that concept does little for me. It doesn't feed me. It has no movement, it's only labeling. With the terms Set Up, Build, and Pay Off, I know exactly what I'm doing in each of those sections. Regardless of genre or length or anything else. What am I setting up and how am I building towards the pay off. There is a lot you will hear about beats: what should happen on this on or that page. For me, that's all painting by numbers and rarely produces original stories that stir you and linger in your mind.

So, based on the information we have from our first five exercises, distilled down into an Idea, we are going to create a Step Outline. Don't get confused between what happens and the explanation of what happens. It is not important why something is happening. It's only what happens that gives you the story structure.

One more thing: Make a choice now. Give your story a title.

Student Exercise Examples

Here's an example from Anja in New York.

```
Step outline
```

```
Set Up
```

Claire gets Tiffany ring from John for their third anniversary.

Claire's friend Emily tells Claire that she thinks the ring is appalling, just one of his confused messages to keep her around.

Claire and John spend a carefree night together and talk about their plan for the future.

```
Build
```

Claire gets an interesting job offer from New York but she tells her boss she has no longer any intention to leave.

John and Claire go on their lunch brake for a stroll inthe park.

They run into John's six year old son Julian, who is there with a friend and the mother of the friend. John introduces Claire as a colleague.

Julian pulls John away to show him something. They all leave and leave Claire alone behind.

Claire tells John that she has a job offer from New York and she is considering it. John is shocked. Claire tells John that she does not want to spend her life as a mistress.

Claire tells Emily that John is finally ready to leave his wife.

```
Pay Off
```

John and Claire get to spend a weekend together .The weekend was planned long in advance.

John learns that his little daughter is in the hospital with severe burns. He becomes edgy. The weekend is a disaster.

Claire watches John's house as he and his family have dinner together.

Claire tells her boss that she will take the job.

Claire gives John the ring back.

That's a good example of an ability to focus the material that Anja had generated in her first five exercises.

Another example—this time from Juha. A soccer-crazy, terrific fellow—and, remember, English is not his first language. This is his Step Outline. There are some loose steps but overall a good start towards the progression of story.

```
Exercise 7 - Step Outline/Juha

SET UP

1. At the stadium Andrea, the goalkeeper, warming up with one
of the players faking missing the ball.

2. At the cafe Sami presents his shortcut to heaven.
Surprisingly, the listener is not Andrea but Luigi.

3. Sergio refuses to join in straight away. He wants to know
Sami´s fundamental motive.

BUILD

1. Sami reminds Andrea the obligation of the settled match:
nothing can go wrong.

2. Sami tries to convince Sergio, who questions Sami´s ethics
and tells there are no shortcuts in life.

3. A prominent sports programme reveals the bigger club is
after Andrea.

4. Sami can´t get in touch with Andrea anymore before the
match.

PAY OFF

1. Emergency meeting at Sergio´s tobacconist´s: how on earth
Andrea will perform?

2. Sami wants more money from Luigi and accuses him to be like
a coward.

3. Sergio points out that Sami is even worse: how can you win
by cheating?

4. They end up at the stadium waving their supporter placards
for Andrea.

5. Andrea makes a magnificent save. We can read the disparate
reactions from the faces of Sami, Luigi and Sergio.
```

All right. We have a basis and progression for the story. At this point, you question your story line. Don't just say, "Oh, I'll work it out as I proceed through the next steps in the process." Tweak it; rewrite it; at the minimum, step back and think about it before moving on. And, yes, we do have two more junctures before we commit to First Draft to focus in even more.

Questioning Your Work

What do I mean by questioning? I mean disengage yourself from the rush that comes with working with your imagination and, inevitably, being seduced by your own Idea. As writers, we have to wear two hats simultaneously. We have to be giddy in the creating and feel the rush flowing through us onto the page. We also have to be objective. Mercilessly detached. What is important going forward for the rest of the process is to be rigorous in developing the habit of questioning your own work. I've talked about it before but now it must become second nature.

Earlier on, perhaps, you worked on impulse and inspiration. Now you've said you want to step up your game. Admirable. So you are learning a process whereby you will be working like a professional. A professional who has developed an understanding, a familiarity with a reliable process that gives you a certain confidence. That confidence allows you to step back and question your own work. Once you've got your story structure, with the Set Up, Build, and Pay Off—with eight or nine, perhaps twelve steps for a short screenplay, and more, of course, for a full length feature—the second part of the exercise kicks in. The Questioning. You must arrive at a place where you are able to trust yourself to question yourself. Don't let someone else tell you what you mean. If it's not clear . . . work on it. Sleep on it. Insist of yourself. Often it is something quite obvious, but in the rush, the sheer pleasure, the fun of it starting to come together, you are blinded to it. Step back. Walk away. It will reveal itself.

If you have every Tom, Dick, and Harry critique your work and give you their opinions, you will fall down the rabbit hole just like Alice in Wonderland!

Now, in my case, when working on material, I find, for some unfathomable reason, that I need to start two steps in front of where I thought I should start. Even when I finish a first draft, I often end up saying, "Wait a minute . . ." and I backtrack. I tell you this to remind you, too, that being a professional writer involves getting comfortable with uncertainty. With change. With fluidity. And, at the same time, also being prepared to make choices and stick with them. It's a complicated business . . . creativity. A messy business with no shortcuts.

Now you might also find as you work that Step 2 and Step 3 are the same step. So combine them. You don't need Step 4 because it's redundant or it's too much information or it gets in the way: Choice. Out! You also have to become comfortable with letting go. Discard stuff you thought was important that as you question now with a critical eye, you know is not. Out! Get rid of it. Not easy because often it's a very good piece of writing, a good turn of phrase but . . . it's getting in the way of the flow. It's distracting. You have to let it go.

So, you see, the questioning becomes very important. After you've questioned your work and made your adjustments you are saying, "This is my outline. At this moment, all things being equal, subject to change . . . this is what my story is."

Evolution of an Idea

It's of value to see how the process works incrementally after questioning. To do this, I have chosen Johanne's script. I want you to see how her first glimpse of an idea (you remember her character, Archie, from Exercise 1) and her character led her to story. She then pieced together all five subsequent exercises and came up with the broad application of an idea.

Johanne did her Idea exercise; then she redid it, based on our questioning it together. She did the same with her Step Outline. It's interesting to see the changes, the evolution of her material.

```
Screenwriting workshop fall 2014 Johanne

Exercise 6: IDEA - Set Up - Build - Pay Off


SETUP
The story takes place in early fall in New York City. Archie
our lead is a widower since 12 years. He lost touch with his
son Andrew when he started dressing in women's clothes and he
is not allowed to see his grandchildren. He spends his days
going to the movie theater and reading newspapers. Until one
day he meets a stranger called Tom.


BUILD
Tom invites Archie over for dinner. The dinner takes a turn
when Tom's wife cuts her finger badly and they have to rush
to the emergency room. Archie finds himself babysitting their
daughter the rest of the night. An odd new friendship develops
between the two.


PAY OFF
Something has happened that night that has an impact on Archie
and leaves his life altered to the better.
```

Johanne made a slight error in her notes here. Her Step 6 as the last step in the Build should have been written as Step 1 in the Pay Off. And she left out the note, "Tom realizes he judged Archie too harshly." When you look at your Step Outline in order to move on to Treatment and then to the script, those things are important to be clear about. Especially when you go to rewrite. The more practice you get the more you will begin to feel them. (The man in the street asked, "How do you get to Carnegie Hall?" The stranger answers . . . Remember?)

Johanne's understanding and adjustments are an excellent example of how the process works.

Screenwriting workshop fall 2014   Exercise 7: The Step Outline
Johanne

Step Outline for "ARCHIE"

SET UP

Perhaps a phonecall

1. Archie listens to a voicemail from his daughter in law thanking him for the gifts he sent his granddaughters. Overmore she apologizes for the fact that her husband Andrew (Archie's son) wouldn't allow Archie at the birthday party.

2. Archie goes to cinema. Here he sees a little girl. A funny moment arise between the two.

3. After the cinema Archie buys a bouquet of flowers and goes to the cemetary to visit his late wife's grave.

BUILD

1. At the cemetary Archie meets a stranger called Tom. Tom initiates a simple conversation that instigates a mutual understanding.

2. A couple of days later Archie receives a phone call from Tom who invites ~~Archie~~ *him* for dinner. *Phonecall with Tom.*

3. Archie goes to Tom's place ~~the day of~~ *for* the dinner. Tom is held up at work and is running late. Tom's 8 year old daughter Emily answers the door. It's the girl from the cinema.

4. Archie and Emily play dress up. While they play they have a heartfelt conversation about their lives. *speak about mother and wife.*

5. Tom arrives home and is flustered when he sees Archie and Emily both wearing make up and woman's accessories (He gets upset because Archie is wearing his late wife's jewelry.)

6. *Tom and Emily speak about Archie.*

PAY OFF

1. It's Halloween and Archie is answering the door handing out candies to kids in costumes. *n is dressed up too.*

2. Archie gets a surprise visit from Tom and Emily and the three of them go Trick-Or-Treating together.

Exercise #7—Step Outline

1. In the form of a Set Up, Build, and Pay Off, write in the specific activities that Set Up the story. Number each step, starting with 1, leaving white space between each step for readability.

2. Do the same with the Build and the Pay Off.

3. Limit each step to a line or two.

4. Write the story down in a logical progression of the key turning points. When I say "logical progression," I do not mean moment to moment. You don't have to write everything that happens.

5. As you fine tune your understanding, you might find you want to misdirect the audience in the Build in order for the Pay Off to work. For now, it is sufficient to simply employ a chronological progression.

6. The Questioning, which is the second half of the exercise, is as important as the first half. Question the logic, your intent, and your imagination. Question your Step Outline to see if your "skeleton" holds up.

7. Rewrite your Step Outline. Every rewrite helps you clarify your work for yourself.

EIGHT

Plotting the Story—I

We've started with Idea . . . we've questioned our Idea . . . we've made some adjustments. Then we went from Idea to shaping the story in the form of a Step Outline. We've said that story is the progression of the significant activities that occur in the telling of the material. Story is what happens—exclusively what *happens*. And we prove out Story by doing a Step Outline. Our Step Outline is the progression of the major turning points in the sequence of what happens. We now have a viable *structure* to our story. So we've gone from generalizing an idea to focusing the Idea into a Step Outline, story structure, a skeleton.

The Step Outline is our reference point as we move into the next stage of process. It's also the most valuable part of the process to go back to when you are doing your rewrites. Know that you might also find you need to change your Step Outline as your story comes more and more into focus for you, the writer. We are still in the architectural stage of our process, and First Draft is still two phases down the line.

Flesh on the Skeleton

So, first, let's talk about Plot. What plotting means is that we are going to take those activities that make up our bare bones structure in your Step Outline and embellish them in ways that make them interesting to an audience. Meaningful, suspenseful, comic or tragic, more dramatic—even misleading, if we want to use a red herring somewhere. We are going to take the skeleton and put flesh and clothing on that skeleton. The kind of flesh and clothing will determine the kind of story we will be telling. Is it a light, frothy story? Does the skeleton have a white suit and white sneakers and a black bowler hat? Is it fun? Or has the skeleton got a big plumed hat and a purple velvet cape? If it is a woman skeleton, is she attractive, stunning, with certain curvaceous appeal? Or is she pudgy and sloppy? How do we dress the skeleton, our story, our Outline, to make it appealing to our audience? That is what plotting is. That is what the clothing on the skeleton does. The Step Outline is the straight through line of

99

the story, whereas the Plotting is all the twists and turns surrounding the through line that make it engaging, intriguing, mysterious, comedic, dramatic, and so on.

The Opening Scene

So let's be more specific about Plot. We can talk about it in the context of the opening scene. The opening scene in a script is likely to sell a screenplay or not. By necessity, the scene has to have an undercurrent of dramatic tension. To illustrate what I mean, I have several examples out of both my work and the work of others. First, I have an example from my script *The Elephant Is Well*. It is a short opening that sets up the rest of the story.

Script Example

```
FADE IN.

EXT: LITTLE ITALY - MORNING

LONG SHOT - Gray, grainy amateur look. It is raining lightly.
We move along a city street. An old woman hurries by with
packages. Kids run by. We move in closer to see POLICELLI a
middle aged fellow in a suit standing on the sidewalk. A short
stocky man named BULL holds a large umbrella over Policelli's
head as he seems to wait.
                    DUBIN - OC
               (anticipatory tones, tense)
          He must be somebody.

An elderly man, Vittorio, moves under the umbrella. He has
on a zippered leather jacket. Policelli and Vittorio smile
and hug.
```

That is a short opening scene. You see all of that. There is no explanation of who they are, why they are there, the background information . . . nothing! What you see is what you get . . . this is what you see. And this is what you hear.

The next example is a fuller example. It's from my script *High Octane*. From my Step Outline I knew I wanted the opening to establish the idea of "oil." So I found a way to dramatize it. Then I knew I wanted to establish my character and the daily operations of a gas station. Juxtaposed against this normalcy, I wanted to introduce the impending crisis: an opening scene that leads into the next part of the story that sets up the scene in the Build.

FADE IN:

EXT. ATMOSPHERIC CONDITIONS - DAWN

Waves of heat, out of focus, forming a kind of mist . . . a
shimmering in the diffused light of early morning. We hear
a lumbering and bursting out of the shimmering waves is the
large front of a tanker truck.

The music over is an anticipatory sound.

                                                CUT TO:

EXT. CITY STREET - EARLY MORNING

The sleek silver and chrome body, bursting forth like some
futuristic iron monster.

                                                CUT TO:

EXT. CITY STREET - EARLY MORNING

The gas truck moves slowly through the deserted city
street. The street lamps are still on and mixed with
the new light of day, the effect is a bit eerie, other-
worldly. As the long silvery truck slows for a red light,
we notice the neighborhood. Old, worn, even in the fresh
emerging
light . . . threadbare.

                                                CUT TO:

EXT. GAS STATION - EARLY MORNING

The gleaming giant gliding into a deserted gas station.

It screeches to a stop in front of the pumps. The driver,
matter-of-factly, climbs down. He stretches.

                                                CUT TO:

Hands expertly fixing a large hose nozzle to a storage nipple.
The hands lock the nozzle in place.

                                                CUT TO:

INT. BATHROOM - EARLY MORNING

Close on water gushing from a faucet in a sink. Hands

scoop up the water.

Follow the hands up as a man washes his face.

                                                CUT TO:

INT. BATHROOM - EARLY MORNING

A medium shot of the man. Hard to tell his age, one of those
faces that remains the same between 35 and 45, nice looking
in a ravaged, working-class way. He splashes water on his
face. We pull back and see that we are in a small bathroom.
Sun beams through the window. We notice a small speaker in the
corner of the ceiling above the window.

                              RADIO ANNOUNCER
                           (Male, authoritative)
                    It's a new day . . . and . . . the spectacle of
                    Arab countries using oil
                              (the man dries his hands and looks up
                              at the loud speaker)
                    . . . as a political weapon hangs over main
                    street as well as diplomatic circles.

                                   MAN
                    Oh shit.

                              RADIO ANNOUNCER
                    Arab members of OPEC, it is rumored, are
                    about to declare an oil embargo against the
                    United States. The long lines at the gas
                    pump . . .
                              (man hangs his head)
                    . . . are certain to continue.

                                   MAN
                              (shakes his head and moans)
                    No . . . no . . . no
                              (turns and looks out window)

                                                            CUT TO:

INT. MAN'S P.O.V. GAS STATION -- EARLY MORNING

Station with gas truck making its deposit. Over we hear that
the radio station has been abruptly changed. Latin American
music blares happily.

OFF SCREEN

                                MAN'S VOICE
                           (Young, smiling sound, no trace of an
                           accent)
                    Hey Boss, your best customer is here.
INT. BATHROOM -- EARLY MORNING

Matt, the Boss, drying his hands as he turns from the window
to face tall, handsome, dark and smiling Paco, the smartly
dressed station attendant, his body dancing in place to the
music from the loud speaker.

                                                            CUT TO:

INT. MAN'S P.O.V. GAS STATION -- EARLY MORNING

Station with gas truck making its deposit. Over we hear that
the radio station has been abruptly changed. Latin American
music blares happily.

OFF SCREEN

                                MAN'S VOICE
                           (Young, smiling sound, no trace of an
                           accent)
                    Hey Boss, your best customer is here.

INT. BATHROOM -- EARLY MORNING

Matt, the Boss, drying his hands as he turns from the window to face tall, handsome, dark and smiling Paco, the smartly dressed station attendant, his body dancing in place to the music from the loud speaker.

BRIDGE . . .

Matt and a pretty little girl play out their charade at the gas pump. He mimes filling her "car" really her bicycle with gas. She mimes paying him and pedals off happy.

Matt attends the long line of cars with the gas he has remaining in the pump.

Ricardo Garcia, a reporter from Action News arrives with his camera crew to get the story from the "man in the street".

That night Matt and Connor, his black partner are on TV. Matt is evasive. Connor is loud.

Fran, Matt's wife is suspicious of Ricardo Garcia who she says only wants to excite his audience.

The next day Garcia is back and wants to feature Matt as the average guy getting squeezed by big oil. Matt is reluctant but Garcia explains the "media event" as the way to attract attention to his problems.

Asks Matt to come with him.

(Continue with scene from the Build)

                                                      CUT TO:

INT: Church - day
Tight on an agitated middle aged priest.

                         FATHER JONAS
          . . . publicity . . . notoriety . . . whoopla
          . . .? Is that what you want us to join?

We pull back and see that we are in a church where a meeting is in progress. We move over the crowd and notice the same neighborhood kids and elders that crowded the garage and swarmed the gas lines watching the drama. They sit aware of the ever-present TV cameras. We see Matt in the front row. We move past them to see Garcia and the serious looking priest up front.

Angle on Garcia as he interrupts the priest.

                         GARCIA
          What are you afraid of? I am Ricardo Garcia.
          You all know me. And yes . . . it is a made
          for TV occasion. Why is there no gas all of a
          sudden? Why are the prices sky high?

(Scene from Build continues . . .)

At the end of the opening scene, you see a chunk of the story progression written in loose compositional form, the *bridge*. That I needed the progression was clear, but exactly how to write it wasn't, yet. So I describe it.

The Bridge

The bridge is the passage between two scenes that are already fleshed out. The bridge is essentially what allows the writer to move forward with the story line prior to committing to first draft. That is what makes Treatment an invaluable tool in shaping your story. More on this in the next chapter.

Another example of an opening scene: this time from the classic John Huston film, *The African Queen*, written by James Agee. It is an example of one of the best opening scenes you'll see. It is not only an opening scene but also a lesson in both Visual Writing and Plotting.

The story goes that James Agee, a well regarded film critic, wrote a profile of golden boy director, John Huston, that was not exactly adulatory. On reflection, he thought he might have screwed up. He had written one screenplay and was trying to break into the film business as a screenwriter. Writing a piece about John Huston was an opportunity . . . and he had been critical. Writers aren't always the smartest, self included. Regretting his misstep, Agee called John Huston with a weak excuse. "It was the editor who had shaped the negative piece . . ." he limped along, no doubt feeling foolish. Huston being Huston, a unique individualist himself, he had admired the writing, so he invited Agee to go hunting. Agee, not a gun man, brought his camera. They were both prodigious drinkers and great storytellers, and the nightly campfires must have been raucous and full of robust laughter. On leaving, Agee said he'd like to try screenwriting. Huston responded favorably. His next project, *The Red Badge of Courage*, a novel by C. S. Forester, was already in the works. But Forester also had a novel called *The African Queen*, which Huston had just bought, and if he, Agee, wanted . . .

The African Queen, now a classic, was written by James Agee in the fall of 1950, with, as stated, "the assistance and cooperation of John Huston." The motion picture was made as an independent production in 1951, for Hougan Pictures. The producer was Sam Spiegel, with John Huston as director, released through United Artists. This film script received an Academy Award nomination in 1952. Humphrey Bogart, for his portrayal as Allnut, received the Award for Best Actor.

James Agee was an intuitive screenwriter hoping to find his way in a new media. His instincts were very good for film. He also was a very good writer who brought the descriptive powers of the best in novel writing to help his new endeavor. He overwrites, but John Huston must have valued his grand displays of verbosity and left it all in. Agee had given Huston all he needed, and more. It was a little overwhelming, long, overwritten in places—what mattered is they were good words. I'm sure they had a profound mutual admiration for each other's talents. It was a case of a trusting and a happy collaboration. It put James Agee on the map as a screenwriter. The opening of the film, almost four minutes of screen time, is without dialogue. Nobody tells you what you the audience, is supposed to understand. We see it roll out on the screen.

The African Queen—*Opening Scene*

```
Ext: A Native Village in a clearing between the jungle and the
river. Late morning.
Long Shot—A Chapel

Intense light and heat. A stifling silence. Then the sound of a
reedy organ, of two voices that make the words distinct, and
of miscellaneous shy, muffled, dragging voices, begin a hymn:
Voices (singing) "Guide me O Thou Great Jehovah . . ."
```

NOTE: For the sake of discussion, I consider the singing of the hymn as sound and not dialogue.

```
Int. Chapel—Long Shot- The Length of the Bleak Chapel, past the
congregation, on Brother, at the lectern, and Rose, at the organ.
Brother, a missionary, faces camera near center: Rose, his sister,
is at side, her face averted. Everybody is singing.
          "Pilgrims through this barren land . . ."

He goes on to describe Rose more closely so that we get a
good look and feel for her. "She too, is singing her best and
loudest, an innocent, arid, reedy soprano; and she too, is
very attentive to the meanings of words:"
          "Hold me with thy powerful hands."

Insert—Halfway through the fore-going line, an exotic and horrible
centipede-like creature slithers into view between two of the
organ keys, without interrupting her playing, as methodically as
she would pull out a new stop, Rose sweeps it away.

Rose—as before—
Completes, "Thy powerful hand."

O.S. Voices of singers unperturbed, Rose finishes her casual
disposal of the bug and pulls out a new stop.
```

NOTE: The action of Rose and the bug might be integrated to occur in description of the action where it belongs. Where it is continuous in the visual flow of the action, no need to return to "Rose as before." It is all of one piece.
   Back to the script.

```
Miscellaneous Shots—
Through rest of hymn, shoot and cut against its lines for
meaning, irony and pathos, roughly as follows,
```

Full view of congregation past Brother and Rose,

Agee then details individual members of the congregation as to
suggested features, expressions and relationships and ends by
saying . . .

These things must be disposed of by late in the first stanza,
which continues.

> "Open now the crystal fountain
> Whence the living waters flow,
> Let the fiery, cloudy pillar
> Lead me all my journey through."

We close on the old dame with the bow singing,
". . . my journey through."

O.S. on ". . . fiery, cloudy pillar," a queer sound, steadily
louder: the absurdly flatulent, yammering syncopation of a
rachitic steam motor. Eyes begin to wander from hymnals:

Cut in Brother frowning and singing louder trying to impose
order; attention to the hymn beings to fall apart a little.
Follow the white, veering eyes to frame through the window.

NOTE: Agee is moving towards using specific visual pictures to tell
his story but remains between the novelist's sense of description and the
specificity of the screenwriter. He is getting closer.

Long Shot—The African Queen.
Whose whistle lets out a steamy whinny, then repeats, with
great self-satisfaction. She is squat, flat bottomed—thirty
feet long. A tattered awning roof in six feet of her stern.
Amidships stand her boiler and engine. A stumpy funnel reaches
a little higher than the awning.
On Second Whinny

Medium Close Shot—
Cut To: Allnut on his boat.

It is Agee who gave me the clues to visual writing. He let me understand
and feel through what I saw. I believed him; I understood where he was
headed when he called for a specific cut and then to the follow shot that
fulfilled the promise of content. I took him seriously when he suggested
that we could describe the visual flow and what happens in the frame of
the picture and then to the progression and flow of pictures to convey
meaning and feeling.

Plot the Opening Scene

The opening scene of a film is all important. You must tantalize and
seduce your audience into following you. Even before an audience sees
your film on the big screen, you must first seduce the producer and the

director who *read* your script. All genres of film call for imagination here. Something is happening that grabs the reader, lures your audience. Depending on the nature of your story, it can be lyrical, it can be provocative, it can be violent; it *must* be compelling. It is the overture that sets the stage for the story you are about to tell.

Student Exercise Examples

We'll look at this example from Nur. Good story, and she worked the visuals in well.

```
Nur Sati
Spoleto - Exercise 8

FADE IN:
INT. SELJUK'S OFFICE - MORNING

We see a LONG SHOT of SELJUK in his office. He is a 53 year
old prominent Turkish businessman in Jordan. He is tall, big
build, but not all muscle though you can tell he was once
athletic. He has blond hair, small purple eyes, a perfectly
round head, an average sized nose and huge nostrils. SELJUK
sits at his desk reading over some material.

We see that his office looks rich, with leather sofas, good
quality wooden desk, and an array of medals and certificates
hanging on the walls.

                                               CUT TO:

A MEDIUM SHOT of SELJUK's PERSONAL ASSISTANT
handing him a paper, which he reads. The PA is in her 30s,
light brown hair neatly done up in a bun and she is wearing a
Massimo Dutti skirt suit.

                                               CUT TO:

A CLOSE SHOT of the letter SELJUK reads from
the Armed Forces that shows a big red REJECT
stamp in the middle.

The top of the text says:
                 Att: Mr Seljuk Mamar, CEO -
                 Mamar Contracting & Trading
                 Co.

                 'We regret to inform you that your proposal
                 to equip the army with 50,000 Hummers was
                 rejected.'

                 Sincerely,
                 Colonel Brigadier Samer Juneh

The camera moves so that we see a CLOSE SHOT of SELJUK's face
in total shock and anger.
```

> SELJUK
> (Shouting to his PA)
>
> Lina, call my lawyer, will you!

The phone immediately rings on SELJUK's desk and he picks it up.

> SELJUK
> (Still shouting)
>
> I lost the bid, can you believe it?

SELJUK is quiet for a moment while the camera follows his free hand and we see that he lights a cigarette with a shaking hand.

                                                    CUT TO:

A MEDIUM SHOT of SELJUK with his hand in the air, gesturing as he shouts:

> The Colonel said they would give me the
> bid . . . I've already bought all the Hummers.
> Listen you've got to get me out of this
> mess . . . I'm coming over.

                                                    CUT TO:

INT.BISSAN SHAMI LAW FIRM - NOON MEDIUM SHOT

SELJUK is hurriedly and distractedly walking in a very long corridor with marble floor. A CLEANING LADY is mopping the floor. SELJUK nearly slips but catches himself. A few steps later he slips and falls flat on his back, hitting his head.

                                                    CUT TO:

INT. HOSPITAL ICU - AFTERNOON CLOSE SHOT

Yasmine, 32, is SELJUK's daughter and a lawyer at Ernst & Young. She has dark hair and brown eyes. She is slim and dressed in a business suit.

She is in the ICU bent over her father's bed whispering to him. We see a CLOSE SHOT of SELJUK's face, peaceful, smiling, eyes open.

> YASMINE
> (Smiling)
> Dad! It's wonderful to have you back! You've
> been in a coma for four days. We are going to
> be leaving as soon as the doctors say you're
> okay and you can go back to business. I knew
> you'd come out of it fast.

SELJUK looks left and right, grabs Yasmine's arm. We see a CLOSE SHOT of SELJUK's serious face turn giddy.

> SELJUK
> (Whispers)
> Listen, you know how they say you can hear things
> while you're in a coma? Well it's true. I heard
> people talking about me. I'll tell you once

we get home, but it's exciting. I'm resigning immediately and I am going to work on this thing. We're going to be richer than ever before.

> YASMIN
> (Wary, hesitant)
> Dad, what people? What did you hear? No one knows you're in a coma. No one, except your lawyer came to visit you and I was there . . . I'm going to call the doctor.

As YASMINE takes a step back to leave, we move to a MEDIUM SHOT and see SELJUK trying to sit up on the bed in a panic.

> SELJUK
> (Alarmed)
> No! No! Don't do that. No one must know. We're in danger. We have to be careful.

> YASMINE
> (As if she's talking to her child)
> Tell me what you heard.

YASMINE approaches the bed again and we see a CLOSE SHOT of SELJUK's smiley face. The camera moves closer to his face. The camera comes closer and closer into his eyes.

> CUT TO:

EXT. NORTH AFRICAN RED SEA - LATE AFTERNOON
LONG SHOT

We see a large sailboat with an Ottoman Turkish flag and a pirate flag on it. The sea is choppy, so there are pirates manning the sails and out and about on this boat.

> CUT TO:

CLOSE SHOT

Two men are talking in the captain's room. One of them is Barbarossa; the other is another corsair.

> BARBAROSSA
> Seljuk must find the stone. It is the only way he will get all these goods. He must find the stone before anyone else does. And he mustn't tell anyone.

> CUT TO:

MEDIUM SHOT of SELJUK in bed and YASMINE bent over him, listening as SELJUK repeats BARBAROSSA's last sentence.

> SELJUK
> And he mustn't tell anyone.

> CUT TO:

We see a CLOSE SHOT of SELJUK's face showing triumph and we move to a CLOSE SHOT of Yasmine's face showing a very worried look.

Now, each time you work on your story is also a time to reassess your story. In the case of Johanne, she could and did improve on her story using what she found through working the process. In her Step Outline, which you saw in the last chapter, she opened her film with her character Archie at home talking to his daughter-in-law on the phone. After questioning her outline together, we decided she should open the film in the cinema instead. So, in her opening scene, to her credit, she enlarged upon the suggested change and had a lovely moment when Archie sees a head bobbing two rows in front of him wearing rabbit ears. And that tied into her Build of the child being Tom's little girl. She had set it up in the opening. Important. That's the kind of logic I refer to. Not commonplace logic but the logic of visual writing. Also to her credit she went on to find that her monologue exercise, which was in her original Set Up, and that she really liked, didn't fit the story anymore, and she just cut it out altogether. That is something else you have to do. Cut stuff that you really like. You have to be objective and see that perhaps some part of your story doesn't work anymore, doesn't fit the rhythm of the story or stops the forward motion of the story, as was the case with Johanne's monologue. So out!

All that comes with questioning your own work. I tell you this to remind you that nothing is ever set in stone. Your work can always be improved on. It is essential that you internalize as you write. You must hear it and see it and feel it. Yes, and there comes the moment when you know you're done. It's a choice you make.

In the exercise for this chapter, we are going to work only on the Opening Scene of the story and the bridge to the next scene. This is the first piece of clothing you are putting on your skeleton.

Exercise #8—Opening Scene

1. From the Set Up in your Step Outline, the established key points of the story progression—the bare bones of the story—select the opening scene of your film. I say "select" because at each stage of the process, you might find you need to change something. So look at your Set Up again. You might find that what you thought was going to be the opening actually comes after what you initially thought was Step 3. Each stage of the process allows you to reassess your choices.
2. Write the scene you select as your Opening Scene in full Film Form, which means calling the Cuts and setting up the Shots.
3. Below that scene (your opening), in either descriptive compositional form or in the form of a list, write the rest of the steps that comprise your Set Up and continue into the Build, up to the scene in the Build that you select as your most important scene. That's where you stop.
4. Now step back and question your Opening. Does it make sense? Does it hold your attention in a compelling way?

As in all the preceding exercises, stay simple. This is not a test of how obtuse or clever you can be. More important is to ask yourself, "Have I written a dramatic and therefore engaging enough opening to my film so that the audience wants to follow me to the end? The director or producer wants to read the rest of the script?"

Make whatever adjustments are necessary.

NINE

Treatment—Plotting the Story—II

Just as we proved out Story by creating a Step Outline that allowed us to organize and question the logic of the progression, we will now do the same thing with Plot. We will prove out plot the way the scientist proves out his experiment or the detective proves out her theory. We will prove out our story in the plotting of our story. That step in the process is called a Treatment. It is the step that precedes your First Draft.

More often than not in my consulting work I am sent scripts that ramble on and miss moment after moment where the story should be, could be, focused . . . without any real grip on a through line or logical progression. The scripts are a full 120 pages—many times, longer—and make no sense. Why? Because the writer skipped the Treatment stage and went straight to the script with the "what comes next" approach. Indeed, the writer might have skipped all the stages and just relied on this thing called "inspiration." If you want to write at a professional level, you have to put the work in. You have to spend the time.

'Treatment' is another code word in the vocabulary of filmmaking. The literal derivation of the term: This is how I am going to 'treat' this material for the screen. That is what Treatment means. If you put a dozen film folk in a room in Hollywood or New York or anywhere else in the world, you'll get twelve different versions of what a Treatment is: It is said to be no more than three pages. It contains no dialogue or description. It contains a minimum story. It has no explanation. It is . . . it isn't . . . it has . . . it hasn't . . . and on and on. There is no recognized, accepted form for the Treatment. It is a swamp. It has been argued for years, with beauty in the eyes of the beholder.

It used to be that a Treatment was a selling tool. Producers actually sold from Treatments. In fact, in a writer's contract, the first stage was usually a requirement to do a Treatment.

The writer gets paid for the Treatment. The producer is saying, "I am paying you. You are a writer for hire which means that I own the material, but here is a novel . . . here is a short story . . . here is a piece of journalism . . . here is an idea that my wife had on a Thursday morning in September. Do a Treatment as the initial part of our agreement." What the producer is looking for is: Does the writer understand writing for film? Is there a story here? How does the writer handle dialogue? Does the Treatment show imagination? Is there a feel for writing for film at all? As we now know, writing for film is very different from writing any other kind of narrative material.

The producer might read the Treatment and you might never hear from that producer again. You find out by reading *Variety* that somebody else is writing this film. Or, if the producer is a decent person, he or she might call you and say, "Listen, I don't really like what you've done and I don't want to ever hear from you or see you again!"

What Is a Treatment?

The Treatment is the crown jewel of the process. Now, what I am talking about is *my* version of Treatment. I stress *my,* because I find the Treatment the ideal testing stage before launching into a First Draft. It is a trial run. The dress rehearsal. It's when I can try out all the turns in my story, add all the flavor. If they don't work, I know they don't work, without having to write the full script to then find out. I prove out my story in this form called Treatment.

It is a hedge against squandering time on draft after draft until you 'get it right.' For me, the Treatment provides the invaluable goal of finding and proving out what the screenplay needs. We have a form that allows us to try out all the ingredients of our film's stew. I can be inventive with flourishes and intricacy of plot, on the one hand. I can also find out—always a crucial eye opener—that I need to change the order in my step Outline. It may have been staring me in the face when I wrote my Outline, but only now that I have filled out the progression in the form of a Treatment does it become clear. Here is where I invariably find that I need to start the film with a scene that I originally thought belonged later in the story. So I move it. I might find I have complicated the story with too many turns. I eliminate the extraneous ones. It is precarious work. The floor of my study is frequently covered in crunched-up balls of paper. But it is the most vital part of the process. Be aware that you can also over plot and, as my wife says, "throw the baby out with the bathwater." Writing a script is a matter of balance, like building an airplane, or it won't fly. This part of my process has helped me, and I think it can help other writers, because it has a logical appeal to it and it makes practical sense, too. It seems like a lot to do at this one juncture, so just to reassure you, know that you still have one more opportunity, the First Draft, to sculpt and chisel before going to your final script.

Connecting the Bridges

So what I am talking about here is what Treatment means to me. We are now going to work with the material we have gathered and use the Treatment as a template prior to committing to First Draft. With the help of bridges, which you had a taste of in the preceding chapter, your Treatment will be the abbreviated short version of the eventual complete longer version. What you, the writer, are saying is: this Treatment contains all of the elements that prove its worth as a screenplay. It contains all the insights into my characters and their relationships and conflicts and dilemmas. I've followed the Step Outline that allowed me to chart all the major turning points in the story. Or, on questioning the Step Outline again, I've shifted and rearranged the activities. The questioning never stops. The Treatment contains a simple plot arrangement. I've developed the plot of the story to try to make it as interesting as I can. I have additional bits and pieces of Dialogue that I have found along the way that further strengthen what these characters sound like: why they are interesting, why they are colorful, why they will hold an audience's attention. I have three entire scenes written in Film Form, the camera's point of view. If you have found some interesting transitions, put them in. Try them.

With the help of bridges, written in compositional style, I am trying out the material in a kind of bastard form. I am doing the locations, I'm doing the progressions, I am doing the dialogue and I'm doing characterizations, I am doing backgrounds, I am doing the surprise . . . and I'm leaving holes for what I as the writer haven't worked out yet in the form of bridges. We write the bridges in where there's a hole that we know we'll go back to and work out. Because we are *writers*, those stretches of compositional form should be written with some degree of artistic and literary skill. This allows for an interesting and smooth read, and allows a little leeway over the problem areas, especially if a producer is involved. What I as the writer want is a clear arc of the story: Where am I going? Have I got a story? Or do I need to flesh it out even more before I go on to writing the First Draft?

So when I talk about Treatment, it is for you the writer to avail yourself of one stage prior to First Draft, in order to step back and question your work in a serious way. You then take those answers and work with them. If those answers include "my opening is too frantic and leaves the reader disoriented for too long before it gets into the rhythm I want for the rest of the story," you know you have to fix the problem. "My dialogue isn't strong enough in that scene." You go back and build up your dialogue where it's weak. You have another opportunity here to contemplate Dialogue. There are many shades to speech. It can be combustible, humorous, compassionate, combative, sarcastic, cruel, street talk, teen talk, kindly, tender. You have hundreds of colors in your palette.

It would be redundant to say that when working on the exercise for this chapter you can expect to take twice the time that you did working on all the preceding exercises. Your primary reason for writing a Treatment is for yourself. You, the writer. Whether you are submitting your Treatment to a producer or not, it is an essential step towards First Draft. I have a lot of people come to me, many of them professional screenwriters, who say they have written ten drafts and still feel—or have submitted their work and been told—their script doesn't work. The Treatment stage will eliminate that frustration. It won't eliminate rejection. The producer or director can relate to the subject matter but still find that the script 'doesn't work' yet. If you use the Treatment stage well you won't end up doing countless drafts. As a writer, you owe it to yourself to write a Treatment.

Basic Dramatic Elements

The director is your ally, so you want to give him or her something to work with. She or he will expand, transport, and visually mine your script for everything it can bring to the film. What you must have in the script that he or she works from is a solid story. Interesting characters; a logical and engaging unfolding of events, with carefully devised, unexpected turns in the plot; and focused, believable dialogue.

There are basic dramatic elements that you need in every story, all stories: romantic comedies, thrillers, adventure, spy capers, science fiction, any story. The characters, the dilemma/s, struggles; the resolution.

1. Characters that are engaging and believable. Be they extraordinary individuals—or individuals with outwardly dull lives, if drawn fully, the audience will relate to them even if they are foreign in nature. The audience will be involved with them from how you write them. Writers with some skill are able to make even the bad guy likeable so the audience is ambivalent, which adds tremendous interest and tension to the story.
2. Situations in which these individuals find themselves challenged in some way. Emotionally, physically, morally . . . whatever. They find themselves in some kind of dilemma or conflict, a struggle that calls for transformation of the main characters. Even the simplest stories have those elements within them . . . simple dilemmas, conflicts, risks.
3. Lastly, an ending that reflects that transformation. It does not have to be a happy ending. Some stories leave you with a question, and that can be a legitimate ending too, provided it has a clear logical basis in the premise of story, in what you have laid into the design of the character. Not just a gimmick or a cop-out ending.

Those parameters are loosely what your Set Up, your Build, and your Pay Off were about. You might find you want to go back to your Idea exercise and see if you have lost something along the way.

Step Back and Question

When we finish the Treatment, we do the same thing I have suggested with all of the previous exercises. We step back and we say, "Ok, I can fool everybody. I can fool the producer because I am a clever writer, I can fool my agent, my boyfriend, my girlfriend. I can't fool myself!" This questioning is between you and you. I hear writers say, "I'm going to show this to my wife to read. She has got a very good ear, she's a good critic." Why? People do it all the time. They give their material to people who don't know what they are reading and who are only too happy to give you an opinion. "The script is too this or that! You should be a dentist." Or with all the best intentions in the world, "Sue, you are a terrific person and I really like you, please don't take this badly . . ." What experience do they have with the written word, with reading screenplays? Do they have the same sensibilities you have? It's treacherous territory. Best not to go there. When I first went in to sign the lease on my New York apartment, which was by city law a designated "professional" apartment, my landlord asked me what qualified me as a professional, what I did for a living. I told him that I was a writer. He barked back, "Everybody that writes a postcard is a writer!" I had to go home and bring him the Broadway contract that I had fortunately just signed with a producer for my first play. I got the apartment.

If you want to be a writer, you have to develop a discriminating approach to writing. Respect it. Train it. Read. Read. Read. See good films. See good theater. Read film scripts. That's not easy because, as I mentioned before, what's available is most likely not the writer's work unless you know the writer or someone on the inside. What I can tell you too is that few producers actually read scripts, they get farmed out to 'readers,' recent graduates of creative writing schools or film schools who have enough background to read a script but have little or no experience beyond that by which to judge its worth. It is an entry-level job. Many of my students have been readers for film companies who, after four or five years on the job, leave the pressure and the low pay and now want a better understanding of what makes a good script. They soon learn how superficial their understanding was.

Speaking of making a living, I get called by both film and stage producers to fix other people's work. A 'script doctor,' they call it. The problems in the scripts are usually that it has a terrific ending, but the whole thing doesn't add up to the ending; or it has a terrific beginning, but it drags in the middle or the ending is flat. So I have to backtrack. Take the whole thing apart.

Questions to Ask Yourself

1. Is my Opening interesting enough, engaging enough, for my audience to feel, "Okay, I'll follow this where it takes me"?
2. Did I reveal the whole story in the Build . . . give it away? Am I keeping the audience wondering and intrigued?
3. Am I clear about what is driving my story? What the undercurrent is? Is it excitement, suspense, lyricism, mystery? Do I have that on the page and not just still in my head?

4. What drives the different characters? Are their emotions and their intentions in conflict? Have I played with those elements enough so that the audience (who are not mind readers) can follow me?
5. Is it plot heavy so I've lost the emotional thread of the story?
6. Is my Ending strong enough? Does it present a resolution to what I Set Up and built out on in my Build? Endings are hard. You need emotional and psychological and visual logic to make a story come alive. Does the end make sense, or have I just tacked on something that feels awkward because it doesn't flow out of the story up to that point?

Now here comes the tricky part: a screenplay must *move*. You must feel an undercurrent of movement throughout the whole story all the time.

6. Have I considered the Descriptions and the Cuts and called the Shots so that I fulfill all of the above *and* have moved the visual progression so that the story will impact the audience the way I want it to?

It's a tall order, I know. But trust me, if you have you done all the previous exercises according to the instructions laid out, you should be close to where you need to be.

Note to yourself: Don't just hear it; see it, too. And, hardest of all, detach yourself so you can be objective in answering all those questions.

Questioning your own work is almost as important as writing your own work. Don't get lost in what others question. Just don't go there until you're ready. When you do, if you do, make sure you consult with a qualified, experienced screenwriter, not just anyone.

Before we go to the Exercise, here are a few examples from students' work that give you a real taste of this hybrid called Treatment. There are some flaws, but overall they are all fine examples. I should mention that they are, as is all the material in this book, protected by copyright.

Student Exercise Examples

To begin, a short extract from Juha's Treatment to cement the concept of the value of the Treatment and how you bridge between two scenes.

```
                                                CUT TO:

CLOSE UP TO ANDREA'S PROFILE

We still hear the echo of the shout. ANDREA covers his face
with his huge gloves as a sign of disappointment. He turns
slowly around and takes the gloves out of his face. When
we see the both ears he looks slightly amused and when his
movement continues so PAOLO can't see his expression ANDREA
smiles, pleased.
```

The first Bridge:

SAMI tells he needs a partner in order to benefit from his
conspiracy. A wise old man SERGIO refuses, so SAMI gets in
touch with LUIGI, who needs money to get out of his mother's
kitchen. Does he bite the illegal chance?

It turns out that LUIGI put all his savings at stake, because
he brings the alerting news in total panic. The rich giant
team comes to see ANDREA´s skills on Saturday's match.

The Bridge is a helpful tool. It is where you might find that you have
too much material. As hard as it is, you have to make choices and toss
some of it. Hard to get rid of stuff you like—but necessary.

An example now of a Treatment for which we saw the Idea in
Chapter Six. Luiz-Antonio was from Brazil and attended a New York
two-week intensive. A talented writer and special person, author of
several books, he had traveled from Sao Paolo to take a course at a
major university in New York, but still felt the lack of actual practical
knowledge so he came to me the following summer. Luiz is another
student who was writing in a foreign language. Always bowled me
over, that. I found among my students at the universities, and among
my private students, that those students who were working in a
foreign language often turned out better work. Perhaps having traveled and made a big commitment, they paid more attention . . . I'll
never know.

Luiz Antonio - Treatment
"AN ART FORM"

FADE IN:

INT./EXT - LIMOUSINE PARKED ON TIMES SQUARE - NIGHT LS -
TIMES SQUARE

Huge screens displaying commercials are everywhere. Among
them, billboards and lights. A mass of people, most of them
families, walk around. We can see a big black limousine parked
by the sidewalk.

> MAN (VO)
> This is a strange, dark type of story. But the
> strangest thing is this: it is supposed to be
> my story. When I was alive.
>> CUT TO:

CU - BORIS

We see a man around his late sixties. Well dressed on a black
suit, well shaped and good looking, he stares through the
window. His hands keep on moving, playing with Tarot cards.

> MAN (VO)
> By the way, this was me. Or at least, I think
> it was me. Boris. Nice name for a Bulgarian.

BORIS keeps staring at the outside.

>   BORIS
>
>   Do I really have to say to you why I despise
>   all of this? Shit! *Govno!* Just look around.
>   All this ignorant people. The billboard says
>   "jump", they say "how high?".

He punches the window.

                                        CUT TO:

BORIS POV

We see people photographing each other, pointing at the
screens, using Mickey Mouse hats and carrying lots of bags.

BORIS (VO)

Oh, you may say: (making a pitched voice) "Boris, look how
marvelous it is, people from all over the world are here".

                                        CUT TO:

CU – BORIS

>   BORIS (CONT'D)
>
>   So what? It only proves my point: morons and
>   uneducated rich people are everywhere, not only
>   in America, *skapa moya* . . . My darling . . .

                                        CUT TO:

MS – BORIS

BORIS leans his head against the window.

>   BORIS
>
>   When we came to this country . . . Remember?
>   After all that training, we came here to get
>   informations. (changing his voice, talking like a
>   soldier) "To fight against our enemies, to destroy
>   the western civilization". Well, I never bought
>   that! I will tell you now: I did it for the art.

BORIS moves his head. Now he looks inside the limo.

                                        CUT TO:

BORIS POV

We see a woman, in an evening gown. Blood is all around her
neck and chest. Her head is bending, she does not move, her
eyes are opened: she is a corpse.

                                        CUT TO:

MS – BORIS AND ANASTASYA

>   BORIS

The art . . . To lie is an art form, *skapa moya*. And I was
doing great until you came back. I couldn't let you destroy my

art. I created this new character, you would have destroyed
it! Sorry to do that to you. Sorry. *Sajaliavam.*

BORIS reaches for ANASTASYA's face and closes her eyes using
his fingers.

                                                    CUT TO:

OVER BORIS SHOULDER

BORIS gets back on staring at the people on the outside. A
group of Japanese, mixed with Africans and Americans, all
acting the same way: they keep on staring at the lights and
the billboards.

                          BORIS

            The whole world has bad taste, Anastasya!

                                                    CUT TO:

CU - BORIS FACE

                      BORIS (CONT'D)

               Stupidity is globalized now. Where is the art?
               Only art can save us.

                                                    CUT TO:

LS - TIMES SQUARE

The Limo drives away. The mass of people keep on acting like
zombies, most of them carrying bags, cell phones, cameras.

                       DEAD BORIS (VO)

               An ex-spy talking about art. I told you this
               was going to be strange.

                                                    CUT TO:

CU - BORIS HANDS

Inside the limo, BORIS plays with his Tarot cards.

                                                    CUT TO:

INT. CHELSEA GALLERY / BORIS' OFFICE - DAY
CU - BORIS HANDS

BORIS plays with his Tarot cards.

We go further and see BORIS seated behind his wooden desk. His
eyes are closed tightly. He takes a deep breath.

                       DEAD BORIS (VO)

               Ok, the Tarot thing. Let me explain. As far
               as I remember, I felt the impulse of creating
               another identity to me. I was retired as a spy.
               I had to use my art, create another self for
               me. C'mon, don't you get tired of your regular
               life?

We go further and now we can see BORIS's whole office. A woman is seating right in front of him. She is wearing an elegant red dress, fancy jewelry, Prada glasses and is on her mid-forties. Her whole body leans in BORIS' direction and she grabs her purse as if it was a life vest.

BORIS places a Tarot card on the table.

                                                    CUT TO:

CU - BORIS FACE

BORIS opens his eyes, staring at the card. He covers his eyes with his hand for a second. Looks at the card again. Nods.

                          BORIS

             See, JENNIFER? This is why I told you I'd not
             use my Tarot cards on you. It is hard for me!

                                                    CUT TO:

MS - BORIS AND JENNIFER

JENNIFER stands up.

                          JENNIFER
                  (begging)

             Please, BORIS, tell me everything. Please. . .

We see BORIS explaining to JENNIFER something really bad is about to happen to her husband, JOHNSON.

JENNIFER gets upset, but tries to give BORIS more money. He refuses it. As the narrator (DEAD BORIS) says:

                          DEAD BORIS (VO)

             And before you have a bad impression, it wasn't
             all about the money. Really . . . I felt like a
             painter, a Kandinsky or a Picasso, admiring his
             new canvas.

The narrator (DEAD BORIS) explains that BORIS's predictions were always accurate because of his old spy's skills. We see BORIS placing a painting in one of his clients' house. Inside the painting, a micro camera is hidden and BORIS, from his laptop, can observe everything that happens inside his clients' bedroom.

After that, we see BORIS in the opening of an exhibition at his gallery. Different people searching for different things on the gallery, but BORIS just wants to do his job: he sabotages one of his clients' car and the man gets seriously hurt.

Then, a major event takes place: BORIS receives a visitor in his gallery.

INT. CHELSEA GALLERY - NIGHT

Boris is at the gallery. Dressed in a black suit and white shirt, he listens to BEETHOVEN'S SYMPHONY No 7 IN A MAJOR, OP 92. The sound comes from a small stereo.

The wooden floor in this part of the gallery is protected,
covered with plastic. Heavy boxes are all over it.

CUT TO:

MS - BORIS

Boris opens one of the boxes and picks up an iron made,
elaborated, sculpture. He leaves it on the floor, admiring
it.

A cell phone RINGS.

CUT TO:

CU - BORIS HANDS

The cell phone is on BORIS hands. We see the name JOHNSON
flashing on the cell screen.

> BORIS
>
> Hi, Johnson. Yeah, still here. You what? At the
> front door? My front door?? Sure, ok. Wait a
> sec, I'll open it for you.

BORIS turns off the stereo. We hear the sound of his FOOTSTEPS.

CUT TO:

LS - GALLERY HALLS

JOHNSON and BORIS walking, side by side. JOHNSON is a fifty
year-old man, Wall Street type of guy. Well-dressed, he tries
to walk firmly and fast, but BORIS keeps his slow pace, making
JOHNSON also slow his pace down a little bit. JOHNSON is
nervous, anxious.

> JOHNSON
> (nervous)
>
> BORIS, Jennifer is out of her mind. She keeps
> on saying this crazy stuff. . .

> BORIS
> (calm)
> All women say crazy stuff.

> JOHNSON
>
> No, she is terrified! Afraid something might
> happen to me. (raises his voice) To me!
> Something violent, you know?

> BORIS
> (calm)
>
> She must have run out of her pills.

> JOHNSON
>
> She said **you** told her these things. That you
> have some sort of magical powers or shit like
> that.

                              BORIS

                    (calm) The Tarot session we had.

                              JOHNSON

                    What the fuck, Boris?! I never thought of you
                    as an ignorant hippie type.

                                                          CUT TO:

MS - GALLERY HALLS

BORIS walks to the area covered with plastic. Johnson follows
him. They step in the plastic.

                              BORIS

                    Sorry I scared Jennifer. That was not my
                    intention.

                              JOHNSON

                    She said something about a bed full of blood, a
                    woman. . .Fuck! What the hell, Boris! Did she
                    pay you for this?

BORIS keeps staring, coldly, Johnson's eyes. He simply reaches the
small stereo and turns the sound on. BEETHOVEN can be heard again.

                          JOHNSON (cont'd)
                           (mad at BORIS)
                    What is this??

                              BORIS
                    Beethoven.

                              JOHNSON
                         (screaming at BORIS)

                    C'mon, I want my money back. Ok, you fooled
                    her. Got your game. Just give back my money,
                    you Russian prick.

                              BORIS
                              (cold)

                    Sorry. What I said to her is true.

                                                          CUT TO:

CU - BORIS AND JOHNSON

BORIS puts his hand on JOHNSON's shoulder, as a friend.

                              JOHNSON
                              (ironic)

                    You gonna tell me you see dead people or
                    something like that?

                              BORIS
(smiling) Well . . . Sometimes I do.

Boris hits JOHNSON's neck.

                                                        CUT TO:

CU – BORIS HANDS

A small knife is at Boris hands. Blood starts to flow
throughout JOHNSON's suit and shirt.

                                                        CUT TO:

MS – BORIS AND JOHNSON

BORIS takes his hand off him. The man lays on the ground,
blood spurt from the wound.

                          BORIS

By the way, I am Bulgarian. Not Russian. Idiot. . . *Tapak*!

                                                        CUT TO:

CU – JOHNSON'S FACE

Johnson gasps, his hand on the wound. He stops breathing.

                          CUT TO:

MS – GALLERY HALL

BORIS starts to walk away. Suddenly, he stops.

                                                        CUT TO:

CU – BORIS

BORIS reaches for a small piece of cloth, right by the side of
a statue.

                     DEAD BORIS (VO)

            You may be thinking: now things got messed up,
            right? Well, they did, but not in the way you
            are thinking.

Blood is all over the art piece. He scrubs the statue gently.
Smiles.

We follow BORIS walking on the gallery, WHISTLING to the
Beethoven tune.

                                                        CUT TO:

On the next morning, BORIS receives a phone call: it is JOHNSON,
the man he has killed the night before. He goes to the gallery
and sees ANASTASYA, the dead woman he was talking to at the
car- she is alive and says her name is LINDA. More: the victim
from his attack at the gallery also shows up with no injuries,
screaming at him, saying BORIS has sold bad art to him.

BORIS, frustrated, tries to go to a quiet place. At the
gallery, he finds a room for thinking.

INT. GALLERY – DAY
CU – BORIS

BORIS sweats, his forehead all wet.

                    DEAD BORIS (VO)

            What happened for real?

                                                  CUT TO:

LS - GALLERY ROOM

A huge art installation, made from metal and mirrors, is
hanging over BORIS's head, on the ceiling. BORIS walks from
one side to another of the room.

                    DEAD BORIS (VO)

            Some people say I was just a mediocre art seller.
            Born on the Queens, son a Bulgarian immigrant,
            with a quiet life. A delusional fella.

                                                  CUT TO:

CU - BORIS HANDS

BORIS pulls one card from his Tarot deck. It is a card where
we can read: DEATH.

                                                  CUT TO:

MS - BORIS

BORIS smiles at the card and throws it away.

                    DEAD BORIS (VO)

            Well, that is not how I remember things. Or how
            I want **you** to remember.

                                                  CUT TO:

CU - TAROT CARD

The Tarot card falls on the floor.

                    DEAD BORIS (VO)

            An artist. That is what I was! A person who
            makes up things.

                                                  CUT TO:

CU - ART INSTALLATION

The rope that held the art installation breaks.

                                                  CUT TO:

LS - GALLERY ROOM

We see the art installation over BORIS head. The huge art
piece bends and makes a CRANKY NOISE. BORIS looks up.

                                                  CUT TO:

BORIS POV

The art installation falls.

```
                    DEAD BORIS (VO)
        Well, truth can be boring. Truth is over rated.

                                        FADE OUT.
```

Luiz lost his way in his story. He has a wonderful imagination enriched, no doubt, by the vibrant culture he comes from. It is better to have an imagination than not—but you can get carried away. You have to reign it in. Luiz got too complicated. Got in his own way. His experience was as a novelist. What's important to note in his exercise is that his Bridges tell him he has far too long a story for a ten- to fifteen-minute short film. That's the value of the Treatment. You don't have to write a full 30-page screenplay for a fifteen-minute film and then have to struggle to cut it back. With a Treatment, you know it while you are writing it, before you waste that time and effort on a first draft that doesn't work. So Luiz had to make a few hard choices to get rid of some of the intricacies in the Plotting.

He also has some Cuts where he doesn't need them. Minor. At first, moving the camera with Cuts and Shots will be clumsy, and that's okay. Once I let the genie out of the bottle, writers get intoxicated by the camera. That's good. That's what I want at this stage. Use the two strings. As you become more practiced, you will know when calling for a Cut is *necessary*. I stress the word 'necessary' because that has to be the justification. When calling a Cut, is it *necessary* to telling your story, not simply a way to state a sequence of visuals?

Let me repeat, the Treatment is at the service of the writer. It is a valuable tool through which to piece your story together as closely as you can before you commit to First Draft. A stage where you can try it out as a whole. A preview of a kind.

Recap—Treatment

Set Up: Who are your main characters? Who are you setting up? It is where you plant the seed of your Idea. What is the germ of the conflict? If it is a comedy, have I established a comic tone? What is it that we are setting up?

Connecting Tissue—Bridge: All the in-between activities, written in compositional form, to the Build scene of your choice.

Build: How am I going to plot the Build based on what I have set up so the audience lets me lead them into the conflict, the dilemma, the challenge, whatever this particular story is about? I am making choices for the audience. I am saying that if the audience follows this line of thinking, this line of understanding, if I have engaged them with my characters, they'll get to where I want them to go by the end of the story. Did I build on the conflict, the dilemma that I set up? Is it clear without holding up signposts? Is it dull? Is it boring? Is it too literal? Have I revealed too much?

Connecting Tissue—Bridge: Written in compositional form up to your chosen scene for the Pay Off.

Pay Off: The pay off is how we bring the audience to this part of the story and reward them with an ending that fits what we have set up and built on. Go back to the structure of a joke. Remind yourself, using the joke as a stereotype of the logical progression of circumstances. Jokes always have a well defined structure with a Set Up, Build, and Pay Off. So, too, must our screenplays move seamlessly, one to the other to the other. Develop your Pay Off with the curls and swirls of plot that hold the audience's full attention until the resolution. You might add a moment of doubt for the character to make it a cliff hanger, give it suspense. The audience is asking: What is he or she going to do? What you are saying is—from this specific set of circumstances in this particular order—my audience will understand and be satisfied with how my story ends.

Take your time with this exercise. Think it through carefully.

Exercise #9—The Treatment

1. You have the opening scene from the earlier exercise.
2. Now, using the Step Outline as your guide, write the connecting tissue (a line or two for each point) between the Opening and a key scene of your choice in the Build. Insert the plot points that you know you will need to fulfill in the First Draft.
3. Write the scene of your choice from the Build in full Film Form.
4. Do the same thing with the connecting material between the chosen scene from the Build, written in full Film Form, and the key scene of the Pay Off.
5. Write the end scene of the Pay Off in full Film Form.
6. Having completed the TREATMENT, step back and question it.
7. Make a note of whatever adjustments you find you need.
8. You will make the adjustments straight into your First Draft.

Take your time.

I think of Irv often, especially when I read scripts. "What would Irv think and suggest here?" He helps me a lot. I owe him a lot . . .
Luigi Ferrara-Santamaria, Producer, Rome

TEN

First Draft Short Screenplay

Audience comes into a theater. People you have never seen before, who don't know who you are. They are going to watch something. They come in full of their own thoughts. About what? About financial problems, about love affairs, about family tangles, about shopping, about anything and everything, they're full of it. And what you say to them is, "All of that stuff. I don't want you to think about that anymore. I want you to stop. And I want you to listen to me. Because I am going to tell you something that you may have heard before, but I am going to tell it to you in a new, unique way, from my sensibility. I am going to tell it to you in this particular order. And because I tell it to you in this particular order, you are going to feel this . . . and you are going to laugh, which was not your intention. And I am going to make you cry . . . which was not your intention. If I am successful in engaging you with the material I present to you in this particular order in this particular way, I will delight you, I will enchant you, I will charm you. I might make you gasp in horror. I might trigger fear. And I will touch you, emotionally. I will move you. I am going to take you away from the concerns you came in with. I am going to do this to you . . . if you listen to me. Now, why should you listen to me? Because I am going to make it interesting and you are going to want to listen to me from the very beginning right through to the crucial moment and the final credits."

What I am saying is that you can tell that from the page. Somebody reading the script for the first time should experience that from the reading. It should be clear from reading the script. The floor plan, the mise-en-scene, should tell you that *this* will get you to that place.

Simply put: You now know how to write for film.

Fulfilling the Treatment

The First Draft ultimately comes down to the nuance of skillful structuring and crafted emotions that we transcribe onto the page in Film Form. It is that technical manual that we end up with that can be given to the creative team on the film, who will now fulfill the intention of the script. Craft is your guide.

Now that you have worked out most of the kinks, the best way to think about writing your script is to sit back and imagine your film is finished, already shot, and in the can. It is being projected onto a wall in front of you. In your mind's eye you look at what's on that wall, you see it, and you transcribe it onto the page. What do I see? Okay, I write it down. What do I hear? I write it down. You have to see it and hear it to write it. It all emanates from you. Your imagination. Your logic. Your barometer for emotion.

The First Draft is where you are sculpting and chiseling. You have many obligations, to yourself and to your work. This is where you fulfill the full potential of your dialogue. Where you enrich it if you find it mundane. It is said that the actress Joan Crawford was on a checkout line at a grocery store in Hollywood when the woman behind her on the line leaned in and said, "Ms. Crawford, why don't you ever play the girl next door?" And Crawford replied, "My dear, if people wanted to see the girl next door they'd go next door." Look back at the chapter on Dialogue. Remind yourself that most of what people actually say is boring. You have to distill it like fine wine. Do your characters all sound like *you*? Or do they reflect the characteristics you said makes them who they are when you described them in the exercises? In the Treatment, you might have realized a couple of your scenes needed to be clearer—or were too clear—again, boring. You dig deeper and find a better way. You made notes. Put them to use now in the First Draft.

The First Draft Screenplay

The most important concern now is logic. Emotional logic, narrative logic, visual logic. The Treatment made clear what you need to still work on to have everything connect, flow, move. Now you have to iron out the muddy parts. The flat parts. Too many films fail because the story sags in the middle. Not necessarily the writer's fault, and one never knows whose fault. Stepping away from your work for a while, a day or two, is a good idea. Disconnect briefly. I say 'briefly' because you never want to be too removed from your material. Stay with it, but put it to sleep for a bit and go do other things. All kinds of questions will come up. All kinds of solutions might surface. In the Treatment, was there at least one surprise? Do you have small nuances of emotion that touch just the right nerve? Was there a moment of humor? If you have written a comedy, is what is comic actually funny? Is it original? Did you mimic or did you find fresh humor in something from your own life? Is there enough texture in your story? Even a short ten- to twenty-minute film has to have all these things. Did the Treatment reveal that you need to build the conflict, the struggle, even more? The moral dilemma. Is your Set Up to the Build clear enough? These are questions that will have surfaced in the Treatment.

I'm convinced that preparation is the key to writing a successful screenplay. The connections with the material that you forge from deep inside you, before you are ready to write. All that fluff and stuff you find. The need to prime the pump and let it all gush out in its own way, is all in the service of preparation to write the screenplay. Everything prior to writing your first draft was preparation. Everything in the bridges has to be fleshed out and written in Film Form. No longer in the prewriting stage, you are at last writing your screenplay, which means it is all in Film Form.

A general rule of thumb is that one page is more or less one minute of screen time. Have you been judicious with calling Cuts and Shots (not overdone it and not just left them out)? I have had students ask, "Irv, can't I just write the script and then put them in later?" No. No. And now I can hear Steve, who made us all laugh with his imitation of me: "Noooo," as he dragged out the vowel. Why no? Because if you don't begin to feel the visual flow of your script *while* you are writing it, if you aren't seeing and hearing it play out in your head as you write it, your writing will be static. There will be no life on the page. You will be leaving it to someone else to breathe life into your story. A dialogue writer who drops in a few lines of description and motivation. That is not Visual Writing. You have now learned how to frame your stories in a visual context.

The final and ultimate responsibility at this point in your work is unity of action. Does your screenplay work as a whole? Apply yourself. The rewards are great. Have fun! If you're not having fun, your work will be stilted and forced. The labor not worth it.

So, as our very own Pay Off, let's look at a few First Drafts. As the saying goes, the proof is in the pudding (or is it in the eating)? Three students, different ages, different backgrounds, different nationalities. With very little additional work, all three of them will have a finished screenplay.

Student Exercise Examples

Here first is young Dovid's first draft. Written in 2014, he is now probably just twenty-one.

```
Dovid S.- First Draft

                    FEELING AROUND

Over we hear a soft calming song is playing over a speaker.

FADE IN

INT - ORTHODONTIST OFFICE - DAY

REUBEN'S POV- A fiftyish balding orthodontist hovers over
Reuben inspecting his face. He pulls the light over
shining it into Reuben's eyes.
```

CUT TO:

MS- Reuben squinting with the lights shining in his face. He has mouth stays and a suction tube in his mouth.

ANOTHER ANGLE- The orthodontist begins, pulling metal brackets out of Reuben's mouth which still has partial braces on.

> ORTHODONTIST
> How old are you, again?

> REUBEN
> (Struggling to talk)
> Seven-Heen

> ORTHODONTIST
> (Sighs)
> What a great age . . . (Lower voice)
> That's when I tried everything . . .

REUBEN looks vastly surprised.

> REUBEN
> Really?

> ORTHODONTIST
> Bo those old memories . . . They're the only things that
> stay with you.
>
> (Lower voice)
>
> Go crazy . . . Except your retainer . . . keep that on.

Reuben gives him a puzzled look.

Another angle - The orthodontist removing the last bit of cement off Reuben's teeth with a drill-like tool. He finishes and starts wiping off the instrument.

> ORTHODONTIST
>
> Rinse.

Reuben picks up a small paper cup, gulps it, gargles and spits out into a mini drain on the side of the chair.

CUT TO:

REUBEN'S POV- The orthodontist is peering down at his mouth eyeing the contents like a fine piece of art. He holds up a mirror.

> ORTHODONTIST
>
> Smile. . .(With satisfaction verging on awe) Magnificent.

CUT TO:

Close up - We move in as Reuben smiles uncomfortably, showing his perfectly aligned set of teeth.

CUT TO:

> (V.O.)MOTHER
>
> (Excitedly)
>
> Let me see!

                                        CUT TO:

INT - CAR - DAY

Close up- Of Reuben's smile in a car visor mirror.

                                        CUT TO:

Medium shot- Reuben is seated in the front next to his mother
in the driver's seat. She is in her forties and maternal looking.
She is smiling broadly.

Reuben gives a smile showing his perfect generic set of teeth.
She lifts his head up with her hand, inspecting all angles of
his smile.

                    MOTHER

              (With great satisfaction)
                    Perfect!

Reuben pulls down the car visor and looks in the mirror smiling.

                    REUBEN

          Thank God that damn bear trap is out of
                    my mouth!

                    MOTHER

          Hey, Mr. No More Braces, do you want to
             celebrate by getting some driving
                    practice.

                    REUBEN

              Hmmmm na. I'm tired . . .

                    MOTHER

          What about your other plans? Are you
          going to do that stand up comedy thing
                 any time soon?

                    REUBEN

          I'm not ready for a live stage yet . . . Could
             you drop me off at Abe's?

The Mother sighs. Puts key in ignition and
starts car.

                                        CUT TO:

INT - ABE'S ROOM - DAY

Medium shot- Reuben is sitting comfortably on the edge of the
bed, Abe, a classically good looking teenager, who lies on his
bed. Abe is under the covers and waking up.

                    REUBEN

          We have to do something tonight! I'm feeling it.

                    ABE

              (Yawns) Feeling what?

                              REUBEN

               That I'm finally going to get some ass.

                               ABE
                           (fake concern)
               You should get that feeling checked out.

                              REUBEN
               (mock laugh) I just got my braces off.

REUBEN flashes his teeth confidently at Abe.

Another angle - Reuben sits up straight and faces Abe.

                              REUBEN

          You know that girl Cindy? From history class?

                               ABE

                    Yeah, the ugly one?

                              REUBEN

     Well, she's having a party tonight, it's at her dads, and ugly
     girls throw the best parties. It's a natural defense mechanism.
                           Let's go. . .!

Abe gives Reuben a reluctant look as if the outcome is
predictable.

     I'm serious. My orthodontist said to go crazy! It's our last
     effing summer before college, and our entire high school career
        we have done nothing crazy and I already regret not having
     anything to regret. . .What am I going to do when I'm old and life
     sucks? I need dirty thoughts to comfort me in my old age. . .
     I've got it all planned out. We'll just crash the party and get
     some love and get out. Ask your brother to drive us, or if that
                    doesn't work we'll just take a train.

                               ABE
               Ok. . .but you have to be cool not like your usual
                          self . . . No
                            farting.

Reuben Turns to Abe with and excited grin.

                              REUBEN

                Abe. . .We are going to experience one of the
                   most coveted pleasures in all of human
                           existence . . .

We slowly move in to a close up.

A smile full of hope and glory starts to emerge on Reuben's face.

                    the reason behind more death than effing war,
                  disease and religion put together . . .! It broke
                  up the Beatles. We are dealing with something
                  extremely profound and poetic. Rapture . . .!
                  Tonight, we will finally understand what life

is about. The universe will open up to us . . .!
This party will be . . .

Reuben's radiant smile fills the screen.

                                            FADE OUT:

                    (V.O.)REUBEN

        the beginning of the rest of our lives . . .!

                    (Quiet)

                                            FADE IN:

EXT - CURB - LATE NIGHT

Fade Into Close up - of Reuben's dejected face.

Hold on Reuben's face. Slowly pull back to see Abe looking
equally dejected. They are sitting on the curb. Abe is wearing
well fitted stylish clothes and Reuben is wearing stylish
clothes that don't fit him right.

                    (Quiet)
                    REUBEN

    I could just jerk off for the rest of my life . . .

                    ABE

            (Softly and sincerely)
    . . . I have to stop hanging out with you . . .

                                            CUT TO:

Close Up - on Reuben's confused facial expression.

                    REUBEN

                What. . .?

                                            CUT TO:

Medium Shot - Of Reuben and Abe. Abe looks away awkwardly.

                    (quiet)

Reuben turns to Abe. His expression sad and serious. Abe
slowly turns to Reuben.

                    ABE

    . . .When I hang out with you, and girls are in the
    picture. . . you're my best friend, but . . . you
                (hard for him) bring me down.

                                            CUT TO:

Close up: of Reuben confused then angry.

                    REUBEN
                (Pissed off)
        . . .Just because we didn't get
                girls . . .

                            ABE

                         (Awkward)

         With girls . . . I'm better off on my own . . .

                           REUBEN

        I'm not going to be your "In the closet friend" . . .! I
                       don't need you . . .!

Reuben jumps up off the curb facing Abe and angrily jabs his
finger.

                           REUBEN

            Don't walk over to my house anymore . . .

                            ABE

                       (Disheartened)

                         C'mon . . .

                           REUBEN

                         FUCK YOU!
                          (Quiet)

Reuben turns his back on Abe. Abe is about to say something,
but thinks better of it, shakes his head, and sighs.

                                            CUT TO:

Medium Shot-A older model Sudan pulls up in front of them.
The front window is rolled down. In the car is a 20 year old
version of Abe.

                          JOSEPH

                      Lez go bitches!

Abe gets up and walks toward the car.

                          REUBEN

                       (Resentful)

              I'm taking the train . . .

                           ABE
                        (sullen)
                      Come on . . .

Abe stands looks meaningfully at Reuben who quickly looks
away. . . Abe shrugs, shakes his head and gets in the car.
The car pulls away leaving Reuben staring blankly. He lets
out a miserable sigh. He sits on the curb looking defeated
and depressed. We slowly pull back as he gazes at the
night sky.

                                            CUT TO:

Close up: of Reuben looking at the sky.

                         REUBEN

If you're listening, please . . . Just Get me laid . . .

                                              CUT TO:

LS - Reuben gets up and starts walking down the dark street.

                                              CUT TO:

MS - A car drives past Reuben and out of view. Reuben looks up
as the car reverses and comes back and stops alongside him.
The window rolls down.

                         JOSH
            Reuben? Remember me from Hebrew school?

                         REUBEN

                  Yeah, yeah Josh.

                         JOSH

            Yeah, yeah. Reuben. What are you doing out here?

                         REUBEN

       I'm coming back from a party . . . Sucked (sighs) I'm heading
                  to the train station.

                         JOSH

       I'll give you a ride, man. I just need to make a quick stop
                         first.

Reuben shrugs, walks to the passenger side of the car.

                                              CUT TO:

EXT - PARK - NIGHT

Long Shot: Two girls walking near the entrance of the park. The
car pulls up to the park and turns off. The girls walk over to
the car

                                              CUT TO:

Medium Shot - Reuben and Josh get out of the car. The girls
approach. One is cute with a bookish attractiveness, this is
Rachel. The other is also pretty and flashy, this is Jessica.
Jessica walks up to Josh and gives him a hug.

                         JESSICA

                  Joshie . . .!

                         JOSH

            (To Jessica)

       Hey, This is my old friend Reuben. I'm taking him to the
                  train after we talk . . .

            (To Rachel and Reuben) We won't be long.

                  (To Reuben)

         You can talk to Rachel . . .

                                  CUT TO:

MLS - Reuben watches them go. Reuben and Rachel stand
awkwardly.

Another Angle - Look at each other. Away . . . Back . . .
away . . . peak and they stand . . . Stand . . . Stand.

                  (quiet)

                  REUBEN

      . . . Oh . . . I'm Reuben . . .

                  RACHEL
                 (straight)
      Rachel. . . but I'm really a Scarlet.

      (and they stand) REUBEN

          Ah . . . Eh

                  RACHEL

          Aaa . . .

      (and they stand) RACHEL

      We should talk about something?

                  REUBEN

    School's safe . . . but who wants to talk about that
           anyway?(pump laughs)

                  RACHEL

     So . . . What are you interested in?

                  REUBEN

    . . . Piracy. I hear there is a lot of money in it.

She studies him . . . Gives him a searching look.

                  RACHEL

    So what do you study in piracy?

                  REUBEN

         Marine biology.

  (They stand and look at each other with a flash of recognition
      . . . slowly a smile emerges on her face.)

                                    CUT TO:

CU - Of her face with that emerging smile.

ECU - Of her fully formed smile.

Overhead we hear a thunderclap.

                    (V.O.) REUBEN

            She smiled . . . She smiled!

                                          CUT TO:

INT - COMEDY CLUB - NIGHT

CU - Stage lights illuminate Reuben's face. He is holding a mic.

                                          CUT TO:

MS - Of Reuben pacing on stage.

                    REUBEN

I could have sworn I heard a thunderclap . . . I knew . . .
something momentous happened. It all started when I
got my braces off. "Perfect" my mother said completely
unbiasedly . . . I'm pretty sure it was because they reminded
her of my grandfather's dentures . . . Still . . . On my last
appointment with my orthodontist he gave me some wistful
advice . . . Go for "it" and make memories because when you
get older they're all you have . . . And I thought I knew
what "it" was . . . I had a quarter life crisis. It put me
through this spiral of regret, anxiety mixed with hormones.
All my memories up to that point were about video games and
porn. What was I going to do without good memories! What was
I going to do in the nursing home! Looking back on a stupid
fucking lifetime of video games and porn! I was missing out
on life! Sex was this force that ran the world! What inspired
Shakespeare! What started wars! What broke up the Beatles!
And I was missing out on it! There was to be a party that
night thrown by an ugly girl. Ugly girls throw the best
parties . . . My best friend Abe and I went and it turned out
to be super shitty. Sitting on the curb after the party . . .
Feeling like turds . . . Abe turns to me "we can't hang out
anymore" . . . He said I was bringing him down and that with
girls he was better off on his own . . . I was in shock.
According to him farting is not proper party socializing . . .
It was like getting disinvited from a birthday party in first
grade. His brother came to pick him up but I couldn't go in
that car . . . Not with my shameful virginity intact. Walking
to the train station thinking about the unrealistic situations
where I might be able to prove Abe wrong an old friend pulled
up next to me. He offered me a ride to the train station.
He said he had to meet his girlfriend and her cousin . . .
Alright, I could do this. We meet up with these two cute
girls. My brain is trying to grapple their inexplicable
beauty . . . He goes off with his girlfriend . . . Leaving
me stranded! Just me and Rachel! STANDING! He set me up
for slaughter! She was cute which made it a million times
worse. . .! What do I say! I was a sweaty mess; parts were
falling off. The silence was killing me! I could only imagine
how she saw me. Just trying on different faces on to hide my
nervousness (make stupid faces). . . She asked what I was
interested in . . . What the hell do I say! What the hell do
we have in common! All there is to my life is comic books, ice

cream and fantasizing about girls . . . My brain is just short circuiting . . . "Piracy . . . There is money in it" was what fell out of my mouth . . . I WAS DEAD IN THE WATER! She just looked at me! Trying to see what kind of weird alien I was. Just when I was about to run away, I heard the thunder clap! She smiled! I was going to live! I even talk to her about my stupid brain malfunctions and she was like ME TOO! After that moment my perspective on teen hood and life changed. I stopped trying to prove Abe wrong because I realized I'm not that guy. The guy who everyone wants to be in high school, the guy who goes to prom, swoons women, has a good time at the beach, and can relate to pop songs. I was OK with that . . . I think I'll be happy when I'm an old man because at the end of the day wisdom comes from the shitty experiences. Sex is just weird and nasty after the hormones go away . . . What I had here was raw human experience . . . I was going to be ok because there was someone who was just as scared as me out there so maybe . . . just maybe . . .

                                                              CUT TO:

CU - Reuben with a hopeful smile.

FADE OUT

This next example is from Juha. It's clear that Juha has a great passion for soccer and an intimate knowledge of the game. It pays to infuse your work with your passion. He could have, for example, been writing a story that involved an intimate knowledge of sailing or coding or a legal case and, if he applied that same kind of personal passion to the fact-based information of that story, he could be as effective. It is the emotion, that underpinning of the story that we are after. And he was flexible enough to use the Italian environment that he was in for the two weeks of the course.

THE GOAL - THE FIRST DRAFT - 12/09/2014 - Juha

We hear sounds like thump . . . thump . . . thump. FADE IN

EXT. FOOTBALL STADIUM - MIDDAY MEDIUM SHOT

We see a football goal bathing in the sun. We pull out and pan right to see two athletes warming up just outside the penalty area where the grass is long and soft. PAOLO, the forward, kicks an easy ball after another towards ANDREA with the sound of thump from the distance of about five meters. They both wear match costume and in addition to that ANDREA wears the training jacket. ANDREA needs just to reach his long arms to their whole length up right or up left to catch the ball. He spits balls to his side and takes immediately a new alert position. It´s an easy practise but it shows that he reacts quickly.

                                                              CUT TO:

ANOTHER ANGLE TO ANDREA

We move along ANDREA towards the goal. While walking he takes
off his jacket and throws it beside the right goal post. He
bends down and finds a sports drink bottle behind the post. He
takes a gulp and throws the bottle on the roof of the goal
against its net.

                                                    CUT TO:

MEDIUM LONG SHOT

We see ANDREA moving in the middle of the goal and getting
ready by crouching a bit. We see that the stadium is an old
one and relatively small. It looks like a stadium for less
than 10.000 spectators. PAOLO sets a ball in the penalty spot
and reverse in order to shoot a penalty. He stops for a moment
to concentrate carefully before running.

                                                    CUT TO:

CLOSE UP TO THE BALL

We see how the forward's support foot emerges beside the ball
and the other one wipes the ball forward out of sight giving a
loud sound like bang.

                                                    CUT TO:

MEDIUM SHOT TO ANDREA

ANDREA dives quickly towards the left lower corner and near
the left post gets his both hands in front of the ball so that
it is thrown away to the side of the goal.

                                                    CUT TO:

ANOTHER ANGLE TO PAOLO

PAOLO waits and receives an easy pass along the lawn from the
direction of the goal with his left foot. He bends down to put
it by hands again on the penalty spot.

                                                    CUT TO:

PAOLO'S POV

We move along PAOLO's POV as he reverses, stands still a
moment, we tilt down to see the ball on the spot and we
tilt up as we move fast forward. We hear the sound of bang
and see how the ball flies towards the right upper corner of
the goal. ANDREA jumps vertically towards the corner just
in time to catch the ball and lands sideways on the lawn.
We move closer to see ANDREA getting up and pressing the
ball against his stomach for a while like a treasure. He
returns it towards the penalty shot by throwing it softly
along the lawn.

                                                    CUT TO:

ANOTHER ANGLE TO PAOLO

PAOLO gets ready a bit longer. He sets the ball down, reverses a bit further away. He dances for a moment on his toes, runs his steps and starts to kick.

                                              CUT TO:

ANOTHER ANGLE TO ANDREA

We see ANDREA hinting obviously wrong way: he starts to move to left but right after the sound of loud bang tries to get back to the middle. Too late. He has played himself off the balance and can´t make it back quick enough. The ball smashes to the goal net tightening it heavily.

                    UNKNOWN MALE VOICE
                  (shouts loud in delight)
              Gooooaaaalll!

                                              CUT TO:

CLOSE UP TO THE BOTTLE

The bottle on the roof of the goal jumps up. We hear the sound of a loud bang when the bottle lands on the net of the roof of the goal.

                                              CUT TO:

CLOSE UP TO ANDREA´S PROFILE

We still hear the echo of the goal shout and loud bangs. ANDREA covers his face with his huge gloves as a sign of disappointment. He turns slowly around and as we see full face his smile widens.

                                              CUT TO:

INT. SERGIO´S TOBACCONIST´S - DAY

CLOSE UP TO A FIST

We hear the bang and see the fist bouncing the table.

                    SAMI (VO)
                  (persistently)

              Can´t you see what a fantastic chance
              this is?. . .like a license to print
              money . . .

                                              CUT TO:

MEDIUM SHOT

SAMI and SERGIO sit at the table.

                    SERGIO
                  (brusquely)

              No . . . You need to understand something
              about life.

SERGIO stands up. We move along him beside the wall. SERGIO
points a huge translucent piggy box more than half of coins
and notes of small nomination.

> SERGIO
>
> There is no shortcuts. . .I started with this
> fifteen years ago. When I´m finished with it, I
> can afford to travel around the world. I don´t
> want to have troubles.

CUT TO:

CLOSE UP TO SAMI

SAMI looks disappointed.

> SAMI
> (impatiently)
> But you could book the trip already
> tomorrow!

CUT TO:

CLOSE UP TO SERGIO

SERGIO hesitates.

> SAMI (VO)
> (persistently)
> You could close the shop and stop drudgery,
> think about that . . . I can assure you, there´s
> no risk at all . . .

SERGIO gets rid of his uncertainty.

> SERGIO
> (decisively)
> The answer is no! . . . Like I said, there is
> no shortcuts, and you will learn it too.

CUT TO:

CLOSE UP TO SAMI

SAMI looks irritable. We pull out to see him taking his cell
phone and dialing.

CUT TO:

INT. LUIGI´S KITCHEN - DAY

MEDIUM SHOT

We hear cell phone beeping and see LUIGI sitting at the table
in the kitchen, which belongs to his mothers. LUIGI eats pasta
carbonara unwillingly. He hasn´t yet finished his portion but
his mother, a fat old woman, pours another huge pile of pasta
over his plate.

> SAMI (VO)
> (through cell phone convincingly)

> I know how it is when you are over thirty
> and you have to live like that. But I have a
> solution for you . . .

We move along LUIGI to the toilet. He bends over the bowl. We
hear him throw up.

>   SAMI (VO CONT´D)
>   (through cell phone temptingly)
>
> What if . . . you could triple your
> savings . . . just like that . . . in one
> night . . .

                                                        CUT TO:

INT. LUIGI´S MOTHER´S APARTMENT HOUSE - NIGHT

MEDIUM LONG SHOT

We see LUIGI opening the outdoor of the building silently
in the moonlight. We move closer to see him lifting heavy
luggage out and closing the door cautiously. His expression is
relieved.

>   SAMI (VO CONT´D)
>   (through cell phone)
> The match is settled, like it´s played
> already . . . You just have to make your
> decision . . .

                                                        CUT TO:

EXT. CAR STORE - DAY

MEDIUM SHOT

We see LUIGI negotiating with the car dealer beside a red
Porsche.

>   SAMI (VO CONT´D)
>   (through cell phone)
> I just need a partner to make us both
> rich . . . so, it´s your choice . . . are
> you in . . . or out?

Luigi shakes hands with the car dealer, who gives him the car
keys. We hear the sound of a sports car.

                                                        CUT TO:

INT. STREET OF ROME - DAY MEDIUM SHOT

The red Porsche speeds up in front of the stadium and we hear
how the engine roars.

                                                        CUT TO:

INT. SERGIO´S TOBACCONIST´S - DAY MEDIUM SHOT

We hear the engine roaring, but the engine starts to choke.

LUIGI looks bewildered bending close to SAMI.

>   SAMI
>   (in astonishment)
>   What did you say?

The sound of engine dies.

>   LUIGI
>   (desperately)
>   AS Roma is after him. It was in the news . . .
>   they come to see him on Saturday
>   . . . oh no . . . all my money . . .

>   SAMI
>   (hastily)
>   Now, hold on . . .

>   (Quiet)

SAMI put his arm around LUIGI´s shoulders. LUIGI shakes.

>   SAMI
>   (reassuringly)
>   Calm down . . . When it´s settled, it´s
>   settled . . . whatever happens, Andrea can´t
>   go back . . .
>   LUIGI
>   (uncertainly)
>   How can you be sure?

>   SAMI
>   (emphatically)
>   He knows the rules of this game . . . it´s a
>   game of win or loose . . . life or death . . .

>   (Quiet)

>   LUIGI
>   (fearfully)
>   What . . . what do you mean?

>   CUT TO:

EXT. OUTSIDE THE STADIUM - DAY

MEDIUM LONG SHOT

We see cars and motor bikes parked in front of the stadium
both sides of the street.

>   SAMI (VO)
>   (nastily)
>   I have it under control . . .

>   CUT TO:

MEDIUM SHOT

Andrea jogs slowly a sports bag on his back over the street
towards his Vespa. It´s a sunny day. He bends to unlock the
motorbike.

                                              CUT TO:

CLOSE UP TO ANDREA´S HEAD PROFILE

We see the clear shadow of a handgun pointing his head
and hear the gunshot. A black hole emerges on his temple
surrounded by blood.

                    LUIGI´S VO
                    (fearfully)
           Would you . . . would you really
           kill him?

More blood spurts from the wound on ANDREA´s cheek. His head
falls out of sight and the smoke of the gun flies through the
screen and fulfils the sight.

                                              CUT TO:

INT. SERGIO´S TOBACCONIST´S - EVENING

A thick smoke of a cigarette disappears and we see SAMI´s
serious face while he exhales the rest of the puff out of his
mouth and nostrils.

                    (Quiet)
                    SAMI
                    (amazedly)
           Are you crazy? . . .

We hear distantly the theme song Eye of the Tiger from the film
ROCKY III.

                    SAMI (CONT´D)
           This is just sports . . .

                    (Eye of the Tiger continues)

                    SAMI (CONT´D)
                    (thinking aloud)
           . . . but . . . it´s not just money . . . I
           would loose everything . . . my wife and kids,
           too . . .

                                              CUT TO:

INT. LOCKER ROOM - EARLY EVENING

                    MEDIUM LONG SHOT

                         (Eye of the Tiger continues)

All the players lay down on their back on the floor on a
circle. Feet towards the center, heads towards the walls. In
the middle of the circle ROBERTO, the coach, walks slowly
around the small table in the middle of the room watching his
team. He stops in front of ANDREA.

                                              CUT TO:

CLOSE UP TO ROBERTO
The volume of the music starts to go down.

                    ROBERTO
        We all know what this match means
        to you, Andrea.
                    (voice trembles with emotion)
        And you can be sure you can trust our support
        . . . like we have always trusted you . . .

CLOSE UP TO ANDREA

ANDREA keeps his eyes shut tightly.

                    ROBERTO (VO)
        It's a great chance . . . and I'm sure you can
        do it . . .

                                              CUT TO:

CLOSE UP TO TABLE
We see a pile of cell phones. One of them sparkles. A
hand takes it.

MEDIUM SHOT TO ROBERTO

                                              CUT TO:

Roberto watches the cell phone on his hand curiously.

                    ROBERTO
                    (laughs hoarsely)
        Andrea, I bet, I bet you want to know
        that somebody's trying to reach you ten
        times . . .
                    (laughs in delight)
        Another big team? . . . They are all after you
        these days . . . Or a big fan of you? . . .
        Maybe you should take it . . . if somebody
        wants to wish you luck.

                                              CUT TO:

ANOTHER ANGLE TO ANDREA

ANDREA stands up, wiping his left eye and heads towards the
shower room.

                    ANDREA
                    (faintly)
        No, I want to be alone for a while . . . to
        focus on the match . . .

                                              CUT TO:

INT. SERGIO'S TOBACCONIST'S - LATE EVENING

MEDIUM SHOT

SAMI and LUIGI sit beside each other on the sofa watching TV.
They have beer cans in front of them.
SERGIO joins in a bottle of imported beer on his hand.

>   SPORTS COMMENTATOR (VO)
> The all eyes are on this man, Andrea
> Botticelli. Is it really a time for him to
> convince AS Roma tonight? We will see it soon,
> the match starts right after the break . . .

>   LUIGI
>   (angrily)
> How is it possible that he doesn´t answer the
> phone?

>   SAMI
>   (furiously)
> It´s so unfair . . .

>   SERGIO
>   (mumbling)
> Unlike bribing the goalkeeper . . .

>   SAMI
>   (hurt)
> Like I had a choice . . .

>   CUT TO:

EXT. FOOTBALL STADIUM – LATE EVENING

MEDIUM LONG SHOT

The referee whistles and the match begins. The bellowing
of the crowd is overpowering. We see ANDREA saving several
difficult shots one after the other.

>   SERGIO (VO)
>   (mimicking SAMI´s voice)
>   No risk at all . . . a chance of a lifetime . . .

>   CUT TO:

INT. SERGIO´S TOBACCONIST´S – LATE EVENING

CLOSE UP TO SAMI

>   SAMI
>   (defensively to SERGIO)
>   You really enjoy this, do you?

>   (Quiet)

>   CUT TO:

MEDIUM SHOT

SERGIO stands up and walks behind his desk.

>   SERGIO
> No, I don´t. But it really should
> be a time for you to face what you
> have done.

>   CUT TO:

CLOSE UP TO SAMI

                    SAMI
                    (tamely)
          You don´t want him to loose? . . . You don´t
          want us to win?

                    SERGIO (VO)
          You think it would be the real win? Can you
          look at the mirror?

                    (Quiet)
SAMI bends his head down. He looks ashamed.

                    SAMI
          You are right . . . I don´t sleep any more, and
          if I do, it´s a guaranteed nightmare . . . If
          he wins, we loose . . . If he loose, we win,
          but it doesn´t feel right anymore . . . I can´t
          win either way . . .

                                                  CUT TO:

CLOSE UP TO SERGIO

                    SERGIO
                    (smiles sadly, mumbling)
          We´ll see . . .

                                                  CUT TO:

CLOSE UP TO FOUR FEET IN FRONT OF THE SOFA

We see SAMI´s and LUIGI´s feet wriggle with excitement. Every
now and then an empty beer can or a cigarette butt appears on
the floor and a foot steps on it.

                                                  CUT TO:

CLOSE UP TO TV SET

WE see a narrow save by ANDREA on the left corner of the goal.

                    SPORTS COMMENTATOR (VO)
          What a save . . . magnificent save once again . . .

                                                  CUT TO:

MEDIUM SHOT TO SOFA

SERGIO celebrates, the others are in shock.

                    Oh no . . .
                    SAMI
                    (astonished)

                    LUIGI
                    (in shock)
          Impossible . . .

                    SPORTS COMMENTATOR (VO)
          It´s just a minute to go and it´s still neal
          to neal and it looks to me that . . . hey,
          watch this, what happened . . . oh no, oh
          no . . .

All three watch the TV amazed.

>   SPORTS COMMENTATOR (VO)
>   Oh yes . . . it´s penalty, that´s what it is
>   and here you can see what happened. It was
>   Andrea Botticelli himself who trips up the
>   forward.

SAMI and LUIGI hug each other, SERGIO stares the television,
eating his fist in shock.

>   SPORTS COMMENTATOR (VO CONT´D)
>   Will the referee throw him out . . . no,
>   fortunately it´s just a yellow card for the
>   goalkeeper. And it´s just half minute left. The
>   penalty will be the last kick of the match, for
>   sure . . .

>   CUT TO:

EXT. FOOTBALL STADIUM - LATE EVENING

MEDIUM LONG SHOT TO THE GOAL

We hear the bellowing of the crowd. The supporters of the home
team stand on the left side of the goal and the supporters
of the away team on the right side. The home team supporters
shouts angrily to the referee while the others celebrate. We
move closer to ANDREA who walks to take his position in the
middle of the goal posts. He looks serious.

>   SAMI (VO)
>   Don´t worry Luigi anymore . . . He knows how to
>   do it . . .

ANOTHER ANGLE

The shooter sets the ball on the penalty spot and reverse.

>   CUT TO:

INT. SERGIO´S TOBACCONIST´S - LATE EVENING

MEDIUM SHOT

LUIGI, SAMI AND SERGIO watch the TV intensively. LUIGI looks
to be in shock tearing his hair. SAMI has a resigned look.
SERGIO takes a short glance at SAMI, then turns back nodding
to himself.

>   LUIGI
>   (almost crying)
>   Mamma mia . . .

>   SERGIO
>   (mumbling)
>   She doesn´t help this time . . .

>   SAMI
>   (sharply)
>   Quiet!

>   CUT TO:

EXT. FOOTBALL STADIUM - LATE EVENING MEDIUM SHOT TO ANDREA

The yelling goes down. We see ANDREA crouching and dancing
slightly still. We hear the whistle by the referee. We see
ANDREA starting to move forward and to left. We hear the loud
bang. ANDREA gets back real quickly to right. He has to reach
with his hands to get the ball and we see the ball flying just
a bit right from the middle point of the goal. ANDREA touches
the ball, but the ball bounces slowly up. The ball has lost
its speed. It falls down and rolls slowly towards the right
lower corner of the goal.

CUT TO:

INT. SERGIO´S TOBACCONIST´S - LATE EVENING

MEDIUM SHOT

LUIGI and SAMI ARE halfway up from the sofa in delight.

CUT TO:

EXT. FOOTBALL STADIUM - LATE EVENING

MEDIUM SHOT TO ANDREA

We see from side of the right goal post, how ball is rolling
towards the corner. ANDREA is still on his toes, in crouching
position staring the ball.

> Gooo . . .

> SAMI (VO)

Suddenly ANDREA dives towards the corner and gets just three
fingers in front of the ball and prevents the score. The ball
bounces to the side . . .

> . . . ooo . . .

> SAMI (VO)
> (chokes loudly)

CUT TO:

INT. SERGIO´S TOBACCONIST´S - LATE EVENING

MEDIUM SHOT

SAMI looks like suffocating. LUIGI hides his face with his
fingers. SERGIO sits still looking astounded, and as the others
falls down SERGIO jumps up and celebrates wildly.

CUT TO:

CLOSE UP TO TV SET

We see ANDREA´s teammates piling up on him and on the
background the supporters of the home team celebrating.

> LUIGI (VO)
> (desperately)
> End of game . . .

```
                         SAMI (VO)
                        (whining)
               End of the world . . .

                         SERGIO (VO)
                        (commandingly)
               Let´s have a drink.
```

```
                                              CUT TO:
```

MEDIUM SHOT TO SERGIO

We move along him behind the desk. He looks pleased, takes a
bottle of Glenlivet and three classes and starts to pour.

```
                                              CUT TO:
```

SERGIO´s POV

MEDIUM SHOT TO SAMI
We see SAMI coming angrily to the desk. On the background
LUIGI lays sideways on the sofa sobbing loudly.

```
                         SAMI
                        (accusingly to SERGIO)
               What´s wrong with you? A time for a toast? We
               have just lost a fortune . . .
```

```
                                              CUT TO:
```

ANOTHER ANGLE TO TWO OF THEM

```
                        (Quiet)

                         SERGIO
                        (shrugging)
               That´s what´s wrong with me . . .

                        (Quiet)

                         SERGIO
                        (softly)
               I´m honest.

               But . . .
                         SAMI
                        (defensively)

                         SERGIO
                        (decisively)
               There´s always a but. I thought you already
               admitted you can´t win either way.
```

```
                                              CUT TO:
```

MEDIUM SHOT TO LUIGI

Luigi stands up in shock. We move along him to the desk beside
SAMI. He takes one of the glass with a generous pour in it.

```
                         LUIGI
                        (admittedly)
```

He´s right, SAMI. It´s over . . . We
were like madmen.

> (Quiet)

SAMI stares Luigi. He nods sadly. SERGIO
watches them in his thoughts.

> SAMI
> (ashamed)
> Mad, yeah . . . Darker than carloads of
> assholes . . .

> SERGIO
> (emphatically)
> Now you´re talking . . . There´s still
> hope in you.

> LUIGI
> (sadly)
> Hope? Doubt that . . . we both are history.

> (Quiet)

SERGIO smells his drink, then taste it. LUIGI
wipes his eye. SAMI rounds his finger around the
edge of the glass.

> SERGIO
> (softly)
> Remember when you set the bet?

LUIGI gives a killing glance to SAMI, who stops circling his
finger. SAMI sighs.

> SAMI
> (in self-pity)
> How can I forget . . . All my savings . . . and
> Luigi´s money too.
> > (turns to LUIGI apologetically)
> Listen, kid, I´m sorry. I shouldn´t bring you
> in this shit.

> SERGIO
> (smiles strangely)
> Well . . . you didn´t . . . actually . . .

> (Quiet)

SAMI drops his glass. We hear it falls to pieces. LUIGI gets
something in to his throat. They stares at SERGIO, then to
each other and back to SERGIO.

What? SERGIO sighs.

> SAMI
> (astonished)

> SERGIO
> (patiently)

You heard me right. You didn´t . . .

                    LUIGI
                    (shouts)
What are you talking about? You . . .

                    SAMI
                    (exited and amazed)
You didn´t set the bet? What the hell for? How
can you do something like that?

                    (Quiet)
SAMI and LUIGI are all ears. SERGIO enjoys
himself for a while.

                    SERGIO
Of course not . . .

SAMI and LUIGI reaches over the desk hug him. SAMI bounces his
back. LUIGI shouts like mad. Then they are astounded again.

                    SAMI
Why on earth . . .

                    (Quiet)

                    SERGIO
                    (thinking himself)
It wasn´t only unfair . . . it was strictly
illegal too . . . I couldn´t accept the bet.
I´m an old man, and I don´t want to spend the
rest of my life in jail . . . I want to travel
around the world, remember?

                                        CUT TO:

CLOSE UP TO PIGGY BOX

It´s still more than half of full coins and bills but there is
a couple of thick bundle of bills too.

                                        CUT TO:

MEDIUM SHOT TO THREE OF THEM

They all look tired. We move along as they go slowly from the
desk to sit on the sofa.

                                        CUT TO:

CLOSE UP TO TV SET

We see how Andrea throws kisses to his fans. His teammates hug
him one after the other and celebrate.

There are camera crews around ANDREA shooing his expressions.

                    LUIGI (VO)
                    (in amazement)
. . . and if ANDREA had lost deliberately?

```
                    SERGIO (VO)
                    (amused)
          Then the money would be here waiting
          for him . . .

                                              CUT TO:

MEDIUM SHOT

All three sit beside each other. They all watch the TV screen.
                    SERGIO (CONT'D)
          . . . but not for you, because I didn't
          set the bet through the computer . . .

SAMI shakes his head smiling astonished. LUIGI
crosses his hands for praying and bends his
head.

                    SAMI
                    (thankfully, turning
                    his gaze to SERGIO)
          Why are you telling this . . . I mean . . .
          You have kept the money . . .

                    SERGIO
                    (smiling sadly,
                    looking back)
          That's what's wrong with me.

                    (Quiet)
          I'm honest . . . and I couldn't have done
          it to that poor boy, Luigi.

                    (seriously)
          But for you? (eyes smiling)
          Maybe . . .

                                              FADE OUT
```

You can see the complexity, the fullness of the story. And it is visual. Mistakes, but all acceptable at this stage. The whole bit with the car is redundant. In defense of this writer, that came from his Transitions exercise, and worked in its isolated form, but he didn't find a way to use it effectively in his First Draft. That's an example of how you can fall in love with what you wrote at some earlier point and are blind to the need later to just get rid of it. It doesn't fit anymore. Not easy, that, for any writer.

Something else to give the writer pause is the frequent use of voiceovers. The way it is, his script would call for the casting agent to be extra attentive in casting extremely identifiable voices so the audience wouldn't be distracted by trying to figure out who was speaking when. Finally, when going to his final script, he might want to find a way to call for fewer Cuts. Students either get Cuts or they don't, and the ones that do, love them, so they get carried away. But good use of the visual. Clearly he could hear and *see* his story. Bravo, Juha. Excellent work.

And finally Donata. Another one who impressed me in so many ways, speaking Italian and writing in English being only one of them. In addition to consulting her dictionary for every second sentence while doing her homework, Donata was up all night writing articles for an online Italian newsfeed that she contributed to. Donata had some experience writing drama for both stage and film in Italy and really blossomed when she came to New York. I'm also pleased to say that Donata just finished her first feature film. It is in Italian, and I'm sure she will have success with it.

```
THE MESS-AGE

SCREENPLAY FIRST DRAFT By DONATA C.

INT. / EXT TERMINI STATION. ROMA: LATE MORNING

LONG SHOT. Film credits (beginning of a movie) superimposed on
the images of the train station.

We see from above traffic in the big station. Platforms full of
people getting on trains or getting off.

                        A SPEAKER
    Train coming from Napoli has just arrived at track 1.

EXTREME CLOSE UP. A big brown suitcase is suddenly opening
on the pavement, nearby the train tracks. Everything is on
the floor. Knickers, socks, t-shirts, etc. A packing of sweet
things babà (typical Italian sweet)

                        OC EMMA

Oh . . . God . . . No!

We see the title: THE MESS-AGE

                                                    CUT TO:


MEDIUM SHOT A girl, whose name is Emma, has just get off the
train; she looks so tired and now she's trying to pick all her
stuff up and to close again her suitcase; breathlessness.

Around her people walking fast in all directions. A man is
getting closer.

                          MAN
                       Need help?

                                                    CUT TO


CLOSE UP Emma is frightened, she looks on the floor while
picking stuff up, without looking at him.

                         EMMA
                    No, I can do it.

                                                    CUT TO

EXT. TERMINI STATION
```

We hear big noises of a big city, traffic, horns.

MEDIUM LONG SHOT Emma is carrying her trolley out of the station. She looks disoriented. Everywhere is crowded.

Camera follows Emma to the street. Men are surrounding.

                    MAN 1

                    Taxi?

                    MAN 2

                    Taxi?

                                              CUT TO

INT. TAXI. LATE MORNING

MEDIUM CLOSE UP Emma is exhausted sitting in the taxi. She is looking out of the windows. It's the rush hour and the car is going too fast.

               A CELLPHONE IS RINGING

Emma finds in the bag the cellphone.

                    EMMA

   Oh . . . finally . . . I'm so tired. Yes, I'm just arrived . . .
                 It's a big mess!

           Yes, now I'm on a taxi.

We see Emma's face. She's confused, she does funny grimaces trying to understand.

                    EMMA

What does it mean, "a legal taxi"? Yellow? . . . with the license exhibited? . . . Just a moment, Dad . . .

                                              CUT TO

Emma's P.O.V. We see nothing is yellow, and there's no license anywhere.

                                              CUT TO

MEDIUM CLOSE UP We see the driver, and behind him Emma is so restless, still hanging up the cellphone.

                    EMMA

           Why it's not yellow?

                    DRIVER

             I hate yellow.

                    EMMA

        And where's the license?

                    DRIVER

Which kind of license?

> EMMA
>
> (loud)
>
> STOP this car NOW!

CUT TO

EXT. ROME. LATE MORNING

LONG SHOT. We see a very trafficked big cross in Roma. Cars and people running everywhere.

Camera holds on Emma standing on the pavement, like a statue, alone with her big suitcase.

1)   INT. AUNT CLELIA'S HOUSE. AFTERNOON

MEDIUM SHOT of a bedroom. The wallpaper is faded, with pink flowers and little birds. There's an old big cupboard, a chair and a little desk. In front of the window there's a bed, a single bed with a high mattress, dominated by Virgin Mary and Child. Everything seems colorless and past.

Emma looks around the bedroom leaning down the suitcase. Close to her, there's an old tiny and slight old woman. She's Aunt Clelia. Clelia crosses herself looking at the Virgin.

> CLELIA
>
> Try to find a room so big now! Impossible!
>
> Furniture? The original ones! 1870!

My grandfather did it . . . but he couldn't get the headline . . .

He died . . . making that cupboard! . . . doggone cupboard . . . But for you is perfect!

Aunt Clelia points at it proudly.

> CLELIA
>
> Do you like it?

CUT TO

MEDIUM CLOSE UP. Emma tries to smile kindly.

CUT TO

MEDIUM SHOT. Clelia comes near the door. Emma is still standing near the cupboard.

> CLELIA

Anyway, I give you a couple of directions: the first one, please don't use the land phone if it's not a need! It's so expensive . . . I never do it and I pay so much! Second: don't walk with heels . . . you know, parquet is so delicate . . . After showering, please leave the door open. Use my kitchen but don't use ever vinegar and lemon on my plates: I'm allergic. And, for the very last time: no one ever smokes in my house. Do you?

Emma just shakes her head.

Clelia smiles, satisfied.

                    CLELIA

   You'll be happy . . . you'll see! Comfortable as a queen!

Clelia closes the door and Emma, exhausted, lets herself
sit on the bed. Then something in front of her captures her
attention.

                                              CUT TO

MEDIUM SHOT. From the corridor, we see Emma show herself from
the door.

                    EMMA

        Aunt Clelia, where's the key of my door?

                                              CUT TO

MEDIUM SHOT. Aunt Clelia wears now a short dressing gown and
slippers with a little pink down, hairpins.

                    CLELA

        Key? I've no keys and you don't need a key!

              We're just me and you!

                  What else?

Aunt Clelia smiles perfidiously.

                                              CUT TO

INT: HIGH SCHOOL "UGO FOSCOLO" - LATE IN THE MORNING

MEDIUM LONG SHOT. Emma walks along the main corridor. She passes
through students, other teachers. All of them look at her up and
down. Emma's clothes look cheaper and simpler then theirs.

                                              CUT TO:

EMMA P.O.V. Students are showing themselves from the door of a
classroom with curiosity. There's writing on the door: "V B".

                                              CUT TO

MEDIUM SHOT. Emma goes straight to that classroom. Students
disappear into the class.

We hear noises of students running, desks, chairs.

                                              CUT TO

INT. CLASSROOM V B LATE MORNING.

MEDIUM SHOT. Emma is standing in front of students.

                    EMMA

            So . . . nice to meet you!

                OFF CAM STUDENTS

> Nice to meet you . . .

                    EMMA

I think you've understood I'm your new biology teacher.

I hope to find a good understanding with you . . . Well, I
have my rules . . . Respect first of all, because I will
                  respect you too . . .

   Ask if you need the restroom . . . Never speak without
                  raising the hand. Ok?

CUT TO:

MEDIUM CLOSE UP. A girl at the first desk whispers into her
friend's ear.

                 A STUDENT

                (whispering)

           I miss Mrs Bertelli . . .

                                              CUT TO:

KNEE SHOT: Emma slowly comes back and sits at the desk. She
puts her signature on the registry.

                                              CUT TO:

CLOSE UP. Emma raises her eyes.

                    EMMA

               Any questions?

                 (SILENCE)

MLS. Students start moving nervously, looking up and down,
looking at cell phones to know what time is it, losing attention.

                                              CUT TO:

MEDIUM SHOT. Emma opens a book.

                    EMMA

    Any desire for this beginning new school year?

              A STUDENT (OC)

           Yes, I have a desire.

                    EMMA

             What's your name?

                                              CUT TO

MEDIUM LONG SHOT. A student from the second desk, with brown curly
hair and a cheeky smile, has his hand raised. His name is Filippo.

                   FILIPPO

Filippo . . . I wish I could have a better experienced biology
teacher . . .

LAUGHS ALL AROUND

                                              CUT TO

CLOSE UP: Emma goes red in an instant.

                     EMMA

   Thank you . . . Filippo. Thank you also in the name of all
            other young teacher like me . . .

              Now, open your book!

                                              CUT TO:

LONG SHOT: Students, noisy, take out the books. Emma is
standing with the book in her hands. She pretends to be self-
confident. She starts reading.

                     EMMA

        When is the origin of human life?

   OVER We hear traffic noises, horns sounding, typical of a big city.

                                              CUT TO:

EXT. VIALE TRASTEVERE. LATE MORNING

              TRAFFIC NOISES AND HORNS

MEDIUM LONG SHOT. A very crowded and noisy avenue in the rush
hour. Emma is walking through people. She's crying.

No one seems to notice her.

                                              CUT TO:

MEDIUM CLOSE UP. Emma looks around confused, without stopping
crying.

OFF CAMERA We hear a phone ringing.

                                              CUT TO:

MEDIUM LONG SHOT Emma is at the end of the pavement, she's
starting to cross the road while searching the phone ringing
in her big bag.

She doesn't see a car arriving fast from the left.

            BIG NOISE OF A CAR HITTING THE BRAKES

The car has stopped now. The driver inside is cursing.
The camera follows Emma, running away, pulling off Viale
Trastevere into a small alley.

                                              CUT TO:

KNEE SHOT. Emma stops nearby a little fountain. She breathes
with difficulty, she wets her hands and her face.

                                              CUT TO:

BIG CLOSE UP. Emma is wetting her face. Her eyes are
closed.

OVER We don't hear more noise of traffic but only her heart beating louder and louder.

                                                    CUT TO

INT. EMMA'S BATHROOM. AFTERNOON.

                    EMMA'S HEART BEATING

CLOSE UP. Emma is completely immersed into the water of her bath. Eyes are closed.

                 A CELL PHONE IS RINGING

                                              CUT TO:

MEDIUM CLOSE UP. Emma surfaces and takes the phone. She looks listless, then she answers joyfully.

                            EMMA

              Oh, Daddy . . . at last . . .

                                                    CUT TO

INT. EMMA'S BEDROOM. LATE AFTERNOON

MEDIUM LONG SHOT of Emma, dressed in a bathrobe and a towel as a turban, walking slowly and suspiciously to her bedroom. Door is open.

                                                    CUT TO

MEDIUM SHOT of Aunt Clelia, who is ransacking Emma's stuff. She opens the suitcase, then reads an agenda, then she holds Emma's cellphone.

                                                    CUT TO

MEDIUM CLOSE UP of Emma standing in the door nervously.

EMMA

Are you looking for something, Aunt Clelia?

                                                    CUT TO

MEDIUM SHOT. Aunt Clelia starts in fear. Immediately Clelia puts down the cellphone, closes the agenda.

                    OFF CAM EMMA

                   May I Help you?

                        CLELIA

                     (embarrassed)

     . . . I'm looking for my glasses . . . I always forget them
                       everywhere . . .

Aunt Clelia is embarrassed. Slowly she raises the hand and touches her glasses, over her forehead.

                    CLELIA

           Oh . . . here they are . . .

                                                CUT TO

LONG SHOT of the room. Clelia walks fast to the door. Emma is
just standing close to the door. Then, as soon as Clelia goes
out the bedroom, Emma closes the door, puts a chair against
the door, and sits down exhausted.

     OFF CAMERA We hear, coming from the corridor, a sound very
          loud. It's RADIO VIRGIN MARY, Vatican's radio.

                  VOICE OF A NUN

     Hail Mary, full of grace. The Lord is with thee.
        Blessed art Thou amongst women . . .

                                                CUT TO

INT. CLASSROOM V B . MORNING

MEDIUM CLOSE UP of a girl chomping gum with arrogance.

                OFF CAMERA EMMA

                 (getting angry)

        What does it mean "I haven't???"

                     GIRL

                  (defiantly)

            It means what I said.

     I haven't homework today. I couldn't do it.

                                                CUT TO

MEDIUM CLOSE UP of Emma writing fast on the registry. Then she
looks at another desk.

                                                CUT TO

CLOSE UP of another girl. She looks shy.

OFF CAMERA EMMA

And what about you? The girl shakes her head, looking down.

                                                CUT TO

CLOSE UP of Emma. She is getting angry but tries to control herself.

                     EMMA

        Who has homework today?

                                                CUT TO

MEDIUM LONG SHOT of the students. No one raises a hand, no one
looks into Emma's eyes. They just look around impatiently.

                                                CUT TO

MEDIUM SHOT of Emma angry. She opens the book and starts writing fast on the registry.

>   EMMA
>
>   Ok . . . You wanted this way . . . As you like . . . For
>   tomorrow: page 66 Exercises 1, 2, 3, 4, 5, 6 . . .
>
>   then at page 67, Exercises number 12, 13, 14, 15, 16.
>
>   OFF CAMERA We hear THE BELL RINGING

>   CUT TO:

LONG SHOT: Students are going noisily out of the class. Emma is taken aback.

>   EMMA
>
>   (Not convinced)
>
>   I write the homework as punishment on the registry!

Camera holds on Emma standing alone now, with the book in her hands.

>   CUT TO

INT CITY-BUS. LATE MORNING

MEDIUM LONG SHOT City-bus is crowded. Emma stands in the corridor. A ticket inspector comes close.

>   INSPECTOR
>
>   . . . Ticket, please . . .

>   CUT TO

MEDIUM CLOSE UP. Emma searches for the pass in the bag. She shows it.

>   OFF CAMERA INSPECTOR
>
>   Thanks . . .
>
>   We hear the inspector's voice going further off
>   Ticket please . . .

Emma is anxious. She is looking for something in her bag . . . something missed. She looks furiously for something.

>   CUT TO

INT. AUNT CLELIA'S HOME. LATE EVENING.

CLOSE UP. Emma is standing, with angry eyes and no laughing at all.

>   EMMA
>
>   (serious voice, articulating the words)
>
>   Where is my *cellphone*?
>
>   I want you to tell me NOW! Don't you say anything?

> Ok, listen to me . . . carefully, because I won't
> repeat it twice.

> What's the problem with me, Aunt Clelia?

> I feel like I'm being spied on!
> I'm not sure . . . but I suppose . . .
> you look also into the keyhole!
> Why are you so curious?

> Give me back my cellphone!

> And give me the key!! My bedroom key!

> Or I will call my father, your beloved grandson,
> and I will tell him you are a THIEF!!

Emma stops to speak and looks around.

> We hear light steps, then silence.

                                                    CUT TO

MEDIUM LONG SHOT of Emma's bedroom. Emma is in front of a mirror.

We hear someone knocking on Emma's door. Emma seems to be petrified. No movements.

> VOICE OVER AUNT CLELIA

> Is everything ok, Emma?

> EMMA

> Yes, Aunt Clelia!

> AUNT CLELIA

> Are you sure about it? I heard you were talking to someone!
> I told you not to use that damned cell phone every moment!

> I'm going to bed . . . and it could be a good idea also for
> you! Goodnight!

Emma now looks angry but she squeezes hands trying to control herself.

> EMMA

> . . . night . . .

                                                    CUT TO

CLOSE UP. Emma looks at herself in the mirror, then turns the light off.

> OVER EMMA

> (whispering) Fuck!

                                                    CUT TO

INT. HEADMASTER'S OFFICE. MORNING

MEDIUM CLOSE UP of a very distinct, elegant man. The headmaster at the desk speaks in a paternal way.

                         HEADMASTER

                    So, what's the problem?

     Are they becoming course, impolite . . . or something else?

                                                      CUT TO

CLOSE UP of Emma. She looks afflicted, her eyes down.

                            EMMA

                     No, not course . . .

                  OFF CAMERA HEADMASTER

                       . . . Then?

                            EMMA

     . . . They act like enemies, since the beginning . . .
       It's like if I stole something to someone else . . .
                          They . . .

                                                      CUT TO

MEDIUM CLOSE UP of the headmaster

                         HEADMASTER

     I know what you mean. Probably they miss their beloved
         Mrs. Bertelli, a wonderful teacher, so sunny, so
                       experienced . . .

     She has gone suddenly . . . a complicated love affair, you
     know . . . Anyway, if they are not impolite, course . . . or
                violent, how can I help you?

       You must find by yourself the right way to conquer the
        audience! Try to be more interesting, attractive, not too
                    strict and boring . . .

                                                      CUT TO

CLOSE UP of Emma's eyes becoming watery.

                  OFF CAMERA HEADMASTER

     . . . You are so young . . . and if you really know that you
     cannot clear a hurdle, maybe you should think by now this is
                  not your job . . . Come on! Ok?

EMMA nods, looking down.

                                                      CUT TO

MEDIUM SHOT. The headmaster takes his cellphone and starts
dialing a number. It's clear he has no more time to spend with
Emma.

                         HEADMASTER

     Let me know how things are getting on! Ok?

You can improve! But you must believe!

                                                     CUT TO

INT TEACHERS OFFICE. MORNING

CLOSE UP. Emma talks to her father by the landline. She's crying
at the telephone, and looks around to see if someone comes closer.

                         EMMA

                       (crying)

         No, Dad! I can't stand it no more!

Please, Dad . . . come and take me . . . I want to come back
                    to San Lorenzello!

Yes, I know! I like teaching but not here! (always crying)

I'm trying to do my best and they keep on humiliating me!

If they only could imagine how I'd like to have fun with
them . . . especially one of them . . . He seems to be
so sensitive and he keeps on hurting me! I hate this
school! I hate this city too! If you don't come, I will
                        run away!

                                                     CUT TO

EXT. TEACHERS OFFICE. MORNING

MEDIUM SHOT of Emma going out the office. She looks shattered.
In that moment she meets Filippo's eyes. He's going to the
restroom. Emma tries to hide her pitiful state.

                                                     CUT TO

VERY CLOSE UP. Emma has still watery eyes. She's embarrassed.

                                                     CUT TO

CLOSE UP. Filippo looks straight in her eyes. There's nothing
threatening in his eyes; on the contrary, he seems to be
sympathetic to her.

                         FILIPPO

              Hi . . . teacher . . .

We hear the bell ringing loud.

                                                     CUT TO

MEDIUM SHOT. Emma runs away. Filippo keeps on looking to her
while he is going to his classroom, among lots of students
talking and kidding.

                                                     CUT TO

INT. A STUDENT'S HOUSE. LATE AT NIGHT

MEDIUM CLOSE UP of a teen girl, long black hair, lying on her
bed smoking a joint. Her name is Serena.

OVER in distance we hear LOUD HARDCORE MUSIC from another room.

Serena looks at the ceiling.

OFF CAMERA A STUDENT

. . . and when will your parents come back home?

SERENA

(in a whisper)

. . . never . . . I hope . . .

CUT TO

MEDIUM CLOSE UP of a boy sitting on a desk, in front of the computer, naked to the waist. He's Roberto. He's chatting with someone, writing fast, and smiling.

OFF CAMERA FILIPPO

What about spaghetti, guys?

CUT TO

MEDIUM SHOT. Filippo is on the door, nearby Serena's bed, drinking a brown beer straight from the bottle.

SERENA

I feel I'm throwing up . . .

Filippo looks to Roberto.

FILIPPO

What are you doin? . . . Facebook addicted! Come on and join me and the others . . .

CUT TO

BIG CLOSE UP of Roberto from his back. We see the desktop. It's a Facebook group "We want Mrs Bertelli back now!" Lots of comments on the wall and photos taken in the class.

OFF CAMERA ROBERTO

(guffawing)

I'm uploading a new photo of that jinxed teacher . . . the new one . . .

Take a look to her shoes . . . where hell does she buy them . . .

CUT TO

MEDIUM SHOT. Filippo stops immediately to drink. Serena looks at him, bored.

FILIPPO

(loud) Don't do it . . . Stop!

SERENA

. . . hey . . . hey . . . .hey . . . be quiet . . .

                                        CUT TO

MEDIUM LONG SHOT of the bedroom. Roberto is not writing and
looks at Filippo.

ROBERTO

Hey? What's come over you, guy?

You're always the first to take the piss out of her! And now???

                                        CUT TO

CLOSE UP. Serena still looks at the ceiling.

SERENA

(confused)

Yes . . . he's right . . . Always pissing out of
                everybody . . .

                                        CUT TO

MEDIUM CLOSE UP of the bedroom.

FILIPPO

Yes, maybe you're right . . . but this time is different . . .
                I mean . . .

SERENA

(laughing)

Are you in love??

Do you wanna . . . yes . . . You know . . .

FILIPPO

(nervously) Don't be silly . . .

SERENA

. . . but she's engaged still now with the Headmaster, didn't
                you say it??

                                        CUT TO

CLOSE UP of Filippo.

FILIPPO

(embarrassed)

. . . bullshit . . . I lied.

                                        CUT TO

MEDIUM LONG SHOT of the room. Serena gets up. Roberto stops writing.

ROBERTO

You lied? . . . Really? Why?

FILIPPO

. . . just a joke . . . I can't 'stand Biology . . . you know
. . .

SERENA

I would have imagine . . . Headmaster is too cool to be
engaged with her . . . but you are a fucking guy!

CUT TO

CLOSE UP of Roberto looking the desktop

ROBERTO

(sadly)

. . . Anyway . . . I miss Mrs Bertelli . . .

CUT TO

MEDIUM LONG SHOT of the bedroom

FILIPPO

Yes . . . me too . . . but it's not new teacher's fault if Mrs
Bertelli left us . . . She had a love affair with a man living
in Milan . . .

SERENA

Oh . . . really? And how do you know about this?

FILIPPO

(smiling)

I know everything . . . remember . . . Be careful! I also
know what you did two hours ago!

CUT TO

CLOSE UP of Serena hiding her face on her pillow laughing.

SERENA

Shit! Shut up!

CUT TO

MEDIUM LONG SHOT of the bedroom. Filippo gives the beer to
Roberto. He drinks.

FILIPPO

. . . and I also think Mrs Bertelli wouldn't appreciate if
she'd knows we are humiliating her substitute . . . at all!

So, remove those photos . . . Roberto is in front of the
computer again. He finished the beer.

ROBERTO

. . . only if you take me another . . .

We hear Roberto burping loud.

                    SERENA

                  (annoyed)

               Oh my god . . .

Filippo is leaving the bedroom

                    FILIPPO

     He was a singer . . . but in another life . . .

                                        CUT TO

INT. AUNT CLELIA'S HOME. EARLY MORNING

MEDIUM LONG SHOT of Clelia's corridor. She's ridiculously
dressed by night, with a little funny pink bonnet. She's
troubled. She's with a man, troubled too. He's about sixty
years old and he looks tired. He's Pietro, Emma's father.

                    CLELIA

     At what time did you wake up???

                    PIETRO

I never slept! She was too shocked by phone . . . I've never
          heard her that way before . . .

Now they are in front of Emma's door. Clelia puts the ear on
          the wood trying to listen.

                    CLELIA

     Nothing! It's not normal at all!

At this time, in the morning she usually sings, then calls
     you, then calls a friend . . . then . . .

Pietro looks straight to Clelia curiously.

                                        CUT TO

CLOSE UP. Clelia is embarrassed.

                    CLELIA

Well . . . I don't do it every day . . . just sometimes . . .

     But today it was a mercy that I did it!

   And I also knocked at the door so many times!!!

   Oh my God . . . (melodramatic) Maybe she feels ill!

              Maybe she's dying????

                                        CUT TO

MEDIUM LONG SHOT of the corridor. Pietro is pushing the door
with his shoulder.

PIETRO

Please, SHUT UP and let me work now!

One . . . two . . . three . . .

Pietro knocks down the door and gets in.

CLELIA

Oh . . . my God . . . another time I've to call that
fucking carpenter! Ohh . . . sorry!

CUT TO

INT. EMMA'S BEDROOM. EARLY MORNING

MEDIUM LONG SHOT of the bedroom. The room is devastated. Clothes
and cigarettes everywhere. On the floor bottles of gin, vodka, beer.

Emma is sleeping, snoring like a tractor. Clelia is paralyzed
at the door.

CLELIA

Oh . . . the Hell!

Pietro tries to shake his daughter.

PIETRO

(loud)

Emma! Emma! It's time to go to school! You're in late, Emma!

CUT TO

MEDIUM CLOSE UP of Emma smiling to her father. She's completely
dead drunk.

EMMA

(speaks and laughs)

HI Daddy . . . Welcome to Jessica Fletcher's house!

CUT TO

MEDIUM SHOT of Clelia. She is upset, removing the little pink
bonnet, mumbling.

CUT TO

MEDIUM CLOSE UP. Pietro is trying to lift up Emma. She's like
a doll, with open arms.

EMMA

Daddy, do you know Aunt Clelia has a poster of Tony Renis
inside her cupboard? And by evening she dances in front of
him singing that fucking song "Dimmi quando quando
quando" I saw her from the keyhole!!! (she dies
laughing loud)

Clelia is embarrassed and upset.

                              EMMA

And . . . and she's also a THIEF! She stole my cellphone!

                              CLELIA

                              (loud)

     NO! Absolutely not! You are too drunk to speak!

                              PIETRO

   Emma, why did you buy all these bottles . . . my God!

                              EMMA

I didn't buy . . . Dad! They were under Uncle Clelia's bed!

Pietro looks at his old aunt, unbelieving.

                                                  CUT TO

CLOSE UP of Clelia, embarrassed.

                              CLELIA

                              (babbling)

     . . . just . . . just . . . when I get a cold . . .

                                                  CUT TO

INT, SCHOOL. MORNING MEDIUM LONG SHOT.

Pietro and Clelia are holding Emma by her shoulder. She can
hardly stand.

                              EMMA

                              (breathing)

              I can't do it, Dad . . .

                              PIETRO

                    Yes, you can!

                              CLELIA

     Pray Virgin Mary and the holy souls of Purgatory.

They will help you, dear! They push Emma into the classroom.

                                                  CUT TO

INT. CLASSROOM V B. MORNING

MEDIUM SHOT of the classroom.. Emma enters walking, trying not
to totter. She looks like a zombie but she's smiling.

                              EMMA

                              (lisping)

              . . . morning . . . guys . . .

                          STUDENTS

                   Good morning, teacher.

Students look into each other's eyes. Emma walks slowly and
throws her big bag on the desk.

                                          CUT TO

CLOSE UP. Serena talks to Filippo's ear.

                          SERENA

                    (in a whisper)

     . . . did she just come back from a happy-hour???

                                          CUT TO

MEDIUM LONG SHOT of the classroom. Emma is looking on the
registry yawning. Students start to smile.

                                          CUT TO

EXT. CLASSROOM. MORNING

MEDIUM CLOSE UP. Aunt Clelia and Pietro are nearby the door.
Aunt Clelia is hearing with her ear on the door. She makes
faces moving the hand like to say "OK!"

                                          CUT TO

INT: CLASSROOM. MORNING

MEDIUM LONG SHOT of the classroom. Emma is sitting on the
chair, with elbows to support her face, trying not to close
her eyes. Filippo raises his hand.

                          FILIPPO

                  Can I talk, teacher?

                          EMMA

                    (still yawning)

             . . . but softly, please . . .

                                          CUT TO

MEDIUM CLOSE UP. Filippo smiles.

                          FILIPPO

             We were wondering if you would like

to accompany us to visit the National Museum of Science next
                          week . . .

                                          CUT TO

MEDIUM CLOSE UP. Emma has just one eye open.

                          EMMA

     . . . because no one else wants to do it, isn't it???

                                          CUT TO

MEDIUM LONG SHOT OF THE CLASSROOM. Students are nodding, smiling. They look friendly now.

FILIPPO

Yes . . . That's true . . . But also because

it could be the right time to know each other . . . don't you?

We would be glad to go with you, teacher!

If you look *now* in the drawer . . .

you'll see the description of the school travel, please!

Emma hardly opens the drawer. She looks interested, surprised.

CUT TO

EXTREME CLOSE UP. Inside the drawer, there's her cellphone. We see also the text message: "Forgive us. Let's start again."

CUT TO

MEDIUM CLOSE UP. Emma closes the drawer noisily. She thinks for a while. Her eyes are closed. Maybe she's sleeping.

CUT TO

CLOSE UP of Emma. She hardly opens one eye, smiling.

EMMA

(yawning loud)

Ok, guys! I'll do it . . . but now, let me think for a
while, ok?

Emma's elbows slide slowly on the desk. Emma falls asleep.

CUT TO

LONG SHOT of all the classroom. Students stand up exulting, or clapping hands, going through the class while Emma sleeps.

STUDENT EXULTING

CUT TO

EXT CLASSROOM. MORNING

Pietro and Clelia exult too.

PIETRO

Good Emma! You got it!

CLELIA

. . . Oh fucking happy day!!!

Old Clelia drinks a little bottle of gin straight from the bottle.

CUT TO

EXT. SCHOOL: MORNING

Pan of the school from outside. Through the window, we see students standing up and going all around. Emma is still sleeping.

```
OVER We hear a song louder and louder "Dimmi quando quando
                        quando"

                    by Tony Renis

                FILM CREDITS THE END
```

We've come a long way. You've climbed and tunneled and soared and trudged. The sock has been turned inside out. If you've come this far . . . done all the exercises . . . questioned each one . . . stayed involved and done all the rewrites . . . you've learned a lot. Like anything, perfecting your skills takes time and takes practice, practice, practice.

Writing is a long process of development. Refining. Honing. Staying with it. Go back and review some of the chapters. Remind yourself. Like a singer doing vocal exercises every morning. Remind your "writer muscles" of the skills you've acquired.

Many writers say they just sit down in the morning and write, never mind what. I don't believe in that. I believe you work on your material every day because you are involved with that material. That you have engaged with that material so it stays with you and insists you give it attention. If you are mid project, if it's a fallow moment, in between commissions, or you simply don't have a compelling idea that you've been developing, do other things. Go for a swim. See good movies. Read good books. You'll find yourself whipping out your notebook in no time to capture the random idea, the flash of a line.

An audience comes to see a film, hoping in their subconscious to find something that alters them, that they were not aware of before; if you write with that in mind, you will write something that matters.

Exercise #10—First Draft Short Screenplay

This last exercise is the culmination of all the prewriting that leads up to the writing of the screenplay. If you have followed the process, including the questioning, at each stage, the First Draft should be close to what you intend your final screenplay to be. You should not need more than two drafts. Having found the places in the Treatment that needed fixing, changing, and making clear notes of what and where to adjust, you follow the "yellow brick road" (from *The Wizard of Oz*) and carry your changes directly into your First Draft.

1. Put all of the connecting tissue that is in compositional form in the Treatment into Film Form. Write the entire First Draft in Film Form. Dialogue, Descriptions, Cuts, Slug Lines.
2. Step back and question your FIRST DRAFT.
3. Fix, adjust, change . . . make your final corrections.
4. Let the cannons roar!

Protecting Your Script

Copyright in the United States

A completed teleplay, screenplay, or stage play may be copyrighted prior to publication or production by submitting on a Form PA.

To request a Form PA (Performance Arts), write to:

The Register of Copyrights
Library of Congress
Washington, DC, 20559

Request the application covering Drama/Performing Arts. The form will indicate the fee that you must send together with a copy of your script.

W.G.A. (Writer's Guild of America) Script Registration

Writers Guild of America offers a unique registration service for members and non-members alike. For a nominal fee, you may register scripts, outlines, formats, or ideas with the Guild. This registration could serve you well in case of future dispute over who had the original idea. Contact the W.G.A. (East or West) for exact registration procedures:

Writers Guild of America East, Inc.
250 Hudson St.
New York, New York 10013
Attn: Registration Department

Writer's Guild of America, West
WGAW Registry
7000 West Third St.
Los Angeles, CA 90048

Alternatively, put the script in a self-addressed stamped envelope, tape seal it, and mail it to yourself. As long as you never open it, that serves as a copyright because it has gone through the Federal Postal Service and will have a dated official stamp on it.

Notes to My Writers

So where have we been together on this voyage? We've been to a continent once known, perhaps, but not familiar. Now, we've taken the main roads and ventured down the side streets. We've met the people. We've been in their homes. We've heard other voices, other tongues, and learned to speak in them. Our imagination is richer. Through skillful use of a new language, the language of film and the tools of the craft, we can express ourselves through the mouths and the sensibilities of our characters. We have learned to do this in motion.

A few things to take away. Make certain your story has good indisputable bones and that the flesh you have clothed it in fits perfectly, propelling the narrative forward to its conclusion. Lyricism is a special quality, and most effective in film, but beware the prose writer's bent toward exposition and reflection, more suited to the novel. It will blunt the dramatic motion in a screenplay.

Stories fail from a lack of material, so you must weave the whole cloth. You cut the pattern out of it later. The pattern, the form you give it, is the screen story. We may not know what is missing, but we know when it's not there. You can always cut down, but you can't cut up. It takes a sort of metamorphosis to become . . . a screenwriter. In the end, you extract only what you need, the essence. You tighten. You sharpen. Take out the water.

In writing for film, the visual is primary and precedes dialogue and action. What we see tells our screen story. So the director is your strongest ally. In the best of all worlds, you will both have the same sensibility, the same vision. Dialogue is only one element by which we tell our story. It is what we see the character do, instinctively, spontaneously, even deviously, crafted by you, as well as how and what they communicate, that shows his or her character and makes the impression on the audience. At times, you use dialogue to simply convey information to the audience, but primarily the purpose of dialogue is for one character to communicate with another: to amuse, to warn, to endear, to intimidate, to distract. The communication must have a believable emotional intention. And though this is hard in the beginning, your characters can't all sound alike. You must dig to find the root of each character's individuality.

Eventually, most important to remember is that the only thing you can be comfortable with is your craft. If you keep practicing your craft, you will find the work becomes easier. Even when you find yourself unsure of where to go next, if you have a craft, you will always have tools to fall back on to move you forward. I don't believe in writer's block. There is always something you can do to put yourself back on track.

Being a writer is a way of life.

Stay with it. If you have the passion you'll find your way.

About the Author

IRV BAUER has mentored many an up-and-coming Hollywood director and writer and is often called upon to consult on screenplays at various stages of pre-production and production, both in the United States and in Europe and Australia. As an educator, Irv taught screenwriting at New York University at the Tisch School of the Arts Film School in the undergraduate school, at The Sarah Lawrence College Writing Institute Extension Program, at the University of Washington, and in master classes at Cornell. He taught playwriting at the University of Bridgeport and the Minneapolis Playwright's Lab at its inception. He also led many a successful non-performance workshop for writers at the New Dramatists in New York.

Irv Bauer is the author of several produced and optioned plays and screenplays, including *The Elephant Is Well*, *Captain of Paradise*, *Hunt*, *Mengele*, and *High Octane*, as well as many commissioned rewrites for film, television, and stage. For the animated series *Courage The Cowardly Dog*, Irv wrote the first season and was Senior Story Consultant on all four seasons.

Among Irv Bauer's many plays are *A Dream Out Of Time*, which was performed at the Promenade Theatre in New York, *A Fine and Private Place*, performed at the Showboat Theater in Seattle, and the musical *Rollin' On The T.O.B.A.*, which had a limited run on Broadway. Some of his other staged plays include *A Ladies' Tailor*, *Cock Of The Walk*, *Bulldog And The Bear*, and *Bullie's House*, which was written in collaboration with the novelist Thomas Keneally.

Irv has taught workshops and seminars on screenwriting all over the world, including a most successful two-week Summer Screenwriting Intensive for fourteen years in both New York and Spoleto, Italy.

Index

Note: Information in figures is denoted by page numbers in *italics*.